INVASION OF THE BODY SNATCHERS

THE MAKING OF A CLASSIC

MARK THOMAS McGEE

Published in the USA by:
BearManor Media
PO Box 1129
Duncan, Oklahoma 73534-1129
www.bearmanormedia.com

ISBN 978-1-59393-288-6

Printed in the United States of America.
Book design by Brian Pearce | Red Jacket Press.

TABLE OF CONTENTS

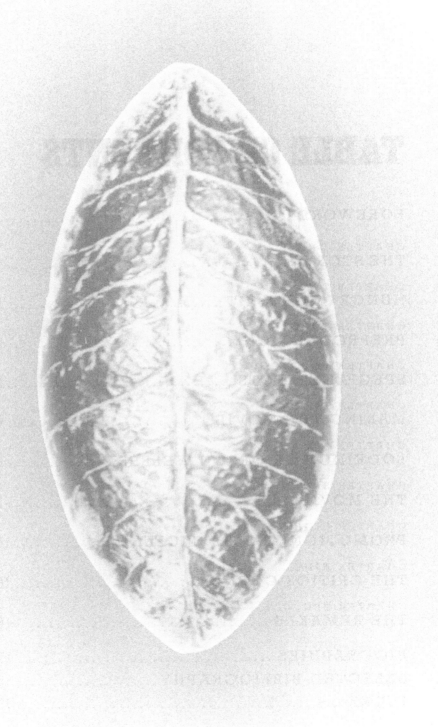

Dedicated to Bill Warren
for making this book possible,
Gary Smith for writing the chapter I didn't want to write,
and to Dave Allen, Kevin Fernan, Ace Mask and Randy Robertson,
all good friends who sat through the picture with me
more times than friendship required.

FOREWORD

All of my film fan friends have a favorite movie and in every case, it's a movie from their childhood. If you think about it, it makes sense. Children don't watch movies—they live them. So the right film at the right age can have a profound and lasting effect on a little psyche. And that movie, whatever it may be, will not be trumped by any other movie, regardless of its quality, content, or sophistication.

Fans return to the movies they love most over and over again until they've drained them dry, hoping to reclaim that initial experience which, of course, they can't. The films have lost their surprise and the viewers have lost their innocence. Still, it's like a visit with an old friend; as warm and comfortable as an old shoe.

My old shoe is the original *Invasion of the Body Snatchers*. I was ten years old when I first saw it and here I am, in my sixties, still talking about it. I'd already seen *Tarantula* and *It Came from Beneath the Sea* (both 1955). The first one scared me so much I left before it was over. Every night, for two weeks, I woke up in a cold sweat from nightmares about spiders. I swore off sci-fi movies for good. I never wanted to go through something like that again. But I had to see that giant octopus destroy San Francisco. Only this time I saw it all, from start to finish with nary a nightmare to follow.

Every morning, I read the movie section of the newspaper. When I saw the advertisement for *The Body Snatchers* I was thrilled by it. People were running from giant, gnarly, alien hands reaching down from the skies to…what? Snatch them I supposed. That's what the title said they did. But what did they do with the people after they'd snatched them? Eat them? Yuck! What if they did something even worse? What *could* be worse? Was I brave enough to find out? Of course I was! I'd seen the octopus movie, hadn't I? I'd passed that bravery test, hadn't I? I was ready. I was ready for *The Body Snatchers*.

Or so I thought.

It arrived at our local theater with a Lucille Ball and Desi Arnez comedy. My mom, being a good sport, said she'd take me but my brother had to go too. It was a Friday night and my dad worked late on Friday and even though my brother was older than me, he was still too young to be left home alone. He wasn't happy about it. He didn't want to see the movie and (more to the point) he didn't want to be seen with his mother and his little brother. The way he carried on you would have thought he was headed for the dentist.

Lucy and Desi were on first. I liked them well enough, but I hadn't come to see them. After the intermission, there were some trailers and a cartoon to sit through. It was like waiting for Elvis Presley to show up on the *Ed Sullivan Show*. Finally, the moment arrived. I sat up in my seat.

Right off the bat the music terrified me. I wanted to jump ship then and there but I couldn't chicken out before the thing even got started. So I sat there and pretended that I was as calm as my mother and brother seemed to be and watched this wild man tell his story. He looked crazy, but I knew he wasn't. I knew that he knew the answers to all of my questions about the Body Snatchers. Was I man enough to listen?

I listened to Jimmy Grimaldi. He said his mother was an imposter. I listened to Wilma Lentz. She said her uncle was an imposter. And I believed them. Some psychiatrist said they were victims of a mass hysteria that had blown through town, but I knew he was full of beans and I had a bad case of the heebie-jeebies. Then they discovered the strange body with no fingerprints and I came to the end of my courage. I asked my mom to take me home, which she was more than happy to do. Not so my brother. He was angry at me for a week. Maybe longer. Who can remember?

For two long years I waited for *The Body Snatchers* to play again. When it did, at a special holiday kiddie matinee, I was there. So was my brother. And (as Ray Harryhausen has so often said about his seeing *King Kong* for the first time) I haven't been the same since.

The Body Snatchers came to Los Angeles television in the early 60s. It premiered on a local CBS affiliate station on *The Late Show*. Of course I wanted to see it again but there was a problem. It was a school night and the movie didn't start until 11:15. On school nights, I had to be in bed by nine. And it was on opposite *Jack Paar*, my dad's favorite show. Fortunately, my brother wanted to see it again too. After a lot of pleading and groveling we got our way. I still remember the little capsule review of the picture that appeared in the *Los Angeles Times* television section that day. It read: "One of those rare, really good science fiction pictures, worth watching all the way."

CBS continued to show the film two or three times a year, alternating between *The Late Show* and *The Early Show* at 4:30 in the afternoon. I watched it every time. But three times a year was not enough to curb my appetite. So I borrowed a tape recorder from a friend and recorded the soundtrack. I had two long play records made from the tape and listened those records until I wore them out. Using high speed 8mm film, I filmed parts of the movie off television and tried to synch the image to my records which proved to be an exercise in futility. (And, as long as I'm being honest about it, stupidity.)

I don't know about you, but when I like a movie, I want everyone to see it. And like it. At the time I didn't know anyone who'd heard of, much less seen *The Body Snatchers*, so it became my mission in life to make sure everyone knew the day and time it would play on television. And I mean *everyone*.

To be a member of our church you had to attend a two-year confirmation class on Saturday mornings. At the end of one of these fatiguing sessions the teacher asked me to stay after class. He told me that I had leadership qualities which he wanted to make use of. He believed that if I'd learn the lessons each week the other members of the class would follow my example. As it happened *The Body Snatchers* was going to be on *The Late Show* the following Friday. "If you'll watch it," I told the teacher, "I'll learn the lesson." He frowned and said that he didn't like those kinds of movies. I told him that I didn't like learning the lessons. So we struck a bargain. He enjoyed it and was sorry that he hadn't let his kids watch it.

A friend of mine (who was once terrified by a truck full of watermelons covered by a tarp) told me that his Boy Scout Troup was going to show *The Body Snatchers*. I telephoned the Boy Scouts and lied to them. I told them I'd been thinking of joining and wondered if it would be possible for me to attend one of their meetings, to see whether I liked it or not. (I know. I know. Shame on me.) It turned out to be one of the best afternoons of my life. Not only did I get to see the movie again, but I found out where I could rent it. No longer would I have to rely on the whimsy of some television programmer. If I could scrape the money together I could see the movie any time I wanted. I was empowered (to use a word that should probably never be used again).

My parents were flabbergasted when I invited the pastor of our church to come to our home to see the film. They were even more flabbergasted when he came. Though my dad was active in the church, the pastor had never been to our home.

Countless screenings followed. My high school Civics teacher and my English teacher came to the house to see it and later agreed to show an abbreviated version of it to their classes. It was also shown to my botany class and my art class. By the time I was done, practically every student in the school had seen the film, some of them more than once. I even showed it to a bunch of delinquents at a juvenile detention center. How that came about I don't recall.

When Dell paperbacks re-issued Jack Finney's novel in 1961, I bought it and read it that same afternoon. But to one obsessed, having a reprint of the novel wasn't enough. Anyone who had return address labels with Dr. Miles Bennell in place of his own name could never be satisfied with a reprint. I had to have the original 1955 edition. And, naturally, I had to have the three *Collier's* magazines in which the serial appeared. That still wasn't enough.

I think I was eleven years old when I started collecting movie stills. I saw an ad in one of the movie magazines for a place called Bruco Enterprises in New York. They sold stills—a quarter for black and whites; half a buck for color. "We've got 'em all!" they boasted so I sent for an eight by ten of Brigitte Bardot who was (and still is) my favorite of the 50s sexpots. Then I started collecting stills from all of the sci-fi movies that I liked. In retrospect, I should have stuck with Bardot because an awful thing happened to me somewhere along the line. I started buying stills from sci-fi movies that I didn't like. Why? To complete the collection of course, whatever the hell that means. Any honest collector will tell you that their collections ultimately collect them.

It should come as no surprise to you when I say that when it came to *The Body Snatchers*, my collecting urges were at a fever pitch. I wasn't satisfied with one or two stills. I wanted them all. One of the best presents I ever got was a special delivery package on Christmas morning from Forry Ackerman, the editor of *Famous Monsters of Filmland* magazine. The package from Uncle Forry contained twenty *Body Snatchers* stills that I had never seen before. I can't think of anything that would have given me more pleasure.

The most famous publicity still from *The Body Snatchers* is the shot of Miles and Becky running from a mob of pod people. There is a street sign visible in that still that ultimately led me to Beachwood and the stairs that Miles and Becky used to escape the pod people. Standing at the bottom of those stairs was an experience like no other. It was magical. For the first time I felt like I was part of the movie and though I had not intended to do so, I was compelled by some strange force to run up those stairs. Miles and Becky were in much better shape than I was. About a quarter of the way up I thought I was going to die. I was wheezing and gasping and my legs felt like rubber. I made it to the top, eventually, but it was at a much slower clip, believe me. And I still thought I was going to die.

Dana Wynter and Kevin McCarthy are pursued by the pod people. This is probably the most often-seen photograph from the movie.

A few weeks later I learned that the cave used in the film was only a few blocks from the stairs, in a place called Bronson Canyon. I know it sounds crazy, but to me Bronson Canyon was more magnificent than the Grand Canyon.

A lady who lived across the street told me that Santa Mira's town square was actually Sierra Madre, a mountain community that was less than twenty minutes away from my home in Arcadia. I couldn't get there fast enough. I would have gone to all of the locations if I'd known where they were. That's the sad thing about film fans. We want to be a part of an event that has already transpired.

One afternoon, Forry Ackerman was kind enough to let me tag along to watch Bert Gordon shoot a movie called *Picture Mommy Dead* at the Doheny Estate. It's a humongous place, built in 1928 by an oil tycoon, and is now (or was) the home of The American Film Institute. One more side note before I get to the point of this story (if there is one). As we entered the room where Bert and his crew were filming, we saw a huge portrait of Hedy Lamarr. She was the mommy in the movie. Miss Lamarr didn't have any scenes that day and when I got home a television newscaster explained how she'd spent her day off. She'd been shoplifting. As a result her part went to Zsa Zsa Gabor. Should you happen to see the movie (which I do not recommend) please note the portrait. They painted Zsa Zsa's face over Hedy's and it doesn't quite look right.

Anyway, Bert was filming a scene with his daughter, Susan, Martha Hyer, Don Ameche, and Wendell Corey. Wendell Corey had the lion's share of the dialog. He gave a performance that effectively sucked the life out of the room. And it was a big room. When he finished Bert said, "That was great, Wendell." One of the grips turned to the photographer and quietly asked, "Was that great?" The photographer blandly replied, "That's what the director said." When I finished laughing I asked someone who the photographer was.

It was Ellsworth Fredericks! He photographed *The Body Snatchers*! Could anything have been better than that?

I cautiously approached him and introduced myself. I told him *The Body Snatchers* was my favorite movie. "It's one of mine too," he smiled. He told me about the trouble they had getting the shot of Kevin and Dana running up those stairs. I don't remember how long we talked before Bert testily reminded Fredericks that they were making a movie. "That," Fredericks said to me under his breath, "is a matter of opinion."

Actually talking with someone who worked on *The Body Snatchers* was a remarkable experience. It had never occurred to me that I could talk to these people. They were Gods. Mortals only spoke to Gods in Greek mythology. But Pandora's Box had been opened and now that I knew it was possible, I wanted to talk to everybody who'd been involved with the making of the film. And the director, Don Siegel, was at the top of my list.

I knew Siegel was making TV movies at Universal at the time so I phoned the studio and asked to speak to him. I didn't think he'd talk to me but what did I have to lose? The operator put me through to his secretary. I assumed she'd politely tell me to get lost but she put me on hold instead. The next thing I knew I was talking to Don Siegel! I was beside myself. I didn't know how much time he'd give me. So I asked him about the scene where Miles, on his way to the kitchen to get some coffee for Jack and Teddy, suddenly fears for Becky's life after Jack says, "Miles, what about Becky? Do you think she's alright?" I asked Siegel if Miles' fear was supposed to be triggered by seeing his own shadow on the wall because it reminded him of Becky's father's shadow coming out of the cellar earlier in the film. "You're the first person that got it!" he exclaimed. "We cut

Kevin McCarthy and Dana Wynter in wonderful Bronson Caves.

that scene every which way but nobody got it." I was feeling pretty special, let me tell you. We chatted for ten or fifteen minutes. I was in Heaven.

I finally met Siegel *and* Kevin McCarthy many years later at a screening of *The Body Snatchers* at The Leo S. Bing Theatre. After the film, Siegel and McCarthy took questions from the audience and remained to sign autographs. I told McCarthy I'd seen the film over a hundred times and started to walk away. "Wait a minute," he said and grabbed Siegel's arm. "Don, this guy's seen the film over a hundred times!" Siegel wasn't impressed. "I've seen it a helluva lot more times than that."

A very dear friend of mine, Randy Robertson, was after me for years to watch the film with him with the sound off. He wanted me to supply the soundtrack. One afternoon at his apartment, after we'd smoked enough weed, I told him that I would do a ten-minute chunk of the picture for him and he chose the greenhouse sequence. I gave him more than he bargained for. I did the dialog *and* the music *and* the sound effects. Before it was over he was laughing so hard he was in tears.

I've don't know how many times I've seen the movie, to say nothing of the number of times I listened to those records. Frankly, I don't want to

This is a reference photograph for the art department. I believe it was taken on the Allied Artists lot.

know. The fact that I know every line and nuance hardly suggests a healthy state of mind. When I was dating my wife, Wendy Wright, the first movie I took her to was *The Body Snatchers*. I also showed her my collection, not that I thought she'd be interested but I wanted her to know what she was getting herself into. Fair is fair. Wendy is a wonderful, cute, intelligent, and extremely capable person. The only blemish on her character is that she married me. I've always been grateful that I didn't get what I deserved.

Had it not been for television it's quite possible that *The Body Snatchers* would be a forgotten film. At the time of its release it was ignored by the major film critics. Now, of course, it has been extensively written about, analyzed, and dissected by an army of film critics and historians who have concluded that the movie is something that it was never intended to be. Jack Finney insists that his story wasn't an allegory of any kind. Don Siegel and Walter Wanger saw it as warning about the danger of conformity. Kevin McCarthy told me he thought it was an attack on Madison Avenue. Walter Mirisch read once that it was an allegory about the communist infiltration of America. In his book, *I Thought We Were Making Movies, Not History*, Mirisch wrote: "From personal knowledge, neither Walter Wanger nor Don Siegel…nor Dan Mainwaring…nor the original author Jack Finney, nor myself saw it as anything other than a thriller, pure and simple."

It's been called a left-wing film, a right-wing film, an anti-Communist film, and an anti-McCarthy film. Call it whatever you like. It's a classic. And I mean classic in the original sense of the word, not just something that's old.

It took a long time but I think it's safe to say that the film has come into its own. In 1994, it was selected for preservation in the United States National Film Registry by the Library of Congress as being "culturally, historically, or aesthetically significant." It's on the American Film Institute's list as the ninth best science fiction film and placed number 47 on their 100 Years, 100 Thrills list of American's most heart-pounding films. It's on *Time* magazine's list of 100 all-time best films. So I am happy to report that after all of this time my love, if not my obsession, for the film has been vindicated.

Obsession is a funny thing. It makes people crazy. I have a friend who is obsessed with finding Western movie locations. He watches movies *for* their locations. He once lived about fifty feet away from the Lone Ranger rock. This same friend had a two-hour video that was nothing but scenes of rocks where Western movies had been filmed. He tried to show it to his lady friend. After ten minutes she told him it was too much butt-crack for her. Without apology, I frankly admit that what you are holding in your hands is butt-crack. It's everything I know about *The Body Snatchers*. And now, like Carswell's parchment, I'm passing it on to you.

THE STORY

*Producer Walter Wanger's "The Body Snatchers" for Allied Artists
established a record in reaching the photography stage 90 days after
the last installment of the story ran in Collier's.*

Allied Artists' Press Release

Jack Finney was in the mood to write a fantasy story. He wanted it to take place in a small town where some sort of a strange event would occur. He kicked around an idea about a dog, injured or killed by a car. An examination of the animal would reveal that part of its skeleton had threads stainless steel running through it. Somehow, the bone and steel had impossibly merged. But Finney didn't know where to go with that idea so he gave up on it and tried another. He wrote a chapter about people who complained that someone close to them was an imposter. He wasn't sure what to do that with that idea either. While he wrestled with it he heard a theory that suggested the pressure of light could push some sort of dormant life through space. By mixing one idea with the other, Finney developed a story that he called *A Rain of Small Frogs*. He sold it to *Collier's* magazine as a three-part serial. The folks at *Collier's* gave it a more provocative title: *The Body Snatchers*.

The first installment of Finney's serial appeared in the November 26, 1954 edition of the magazine. It begins in the office of a 28-year-old doctor named Miles Boise Bennell who resides in the small, northern California town of Santa Mira. His nurse has gone home for the evening and he has one foot out the door when Becky Driscoll, his high school sweetheart, shows up. They haven't seen each other for five or six years. After high school she'd gone to work in Chicago and Miles was off at medical school. Both had married and divorced.

The reason for Becky's visit is her cousin, Wilma who is convinced that her Uncle Ira is an imposter. Becky wants Miles to see if he can talk some sense into her.

Wilma tells Miles that in every way — mannerisms, memories, scars — he seems to be Ira but she's certain that he isn't. In a moment of frustration, Miles points out that her Aunt Aleda couldn't be fooled and Wilma, in tears, tells him that she's an imposter too. Miles persuades her to see Dr. Manfred Kaufman, a psychiatrist.

Before the week is up Miles has sent five more patients to Mannie, all claiming their loved ones are imposters. Manny tells Miles it's the first contagious neurosis he's ever seen. But when Miles' friend, Jack Belicec, shows him something that he found in his basement closet, Miles suspects there's something far more sinister afoot than a mental disorder.

In Jack's basement, on his pool table, bathed in the harsh light of a 150-watt bulb, is a naked body. But it isn't a normal body. There are no signs of rigor mortis, scars, blemishes, or fingerprints. And it's Jack's size and weight. Wondering if there's some connection between the strange body and the delusion that's sweeping through Santa Mira, Miles persuades Jack and his wife, Teddy, to keep an eye on the thing. When Miles takes Becky home she bursts into tears and tells him that she thinks her father is an imposter too.

Later that night the Belicecs show up at Miles' house, Teddy wild-eyed and hysterical, Jack grimly calm. While Jack slept, Teddy had gone to the basement to check on the body. Jack couldn't say what she'd seen because he had to get her out of the house before she went out of her mind but both he and Miles think they know what she saw. Miles phones Manny and asks him to come to the house. And then, remembering what Becky had said about her father, Miles races to the Driscoll home. He breaks into the cellar and finds an unfinished, vague, and indefinite duplicate of Becky. Upstairs he finds Becky asleep and isn't able to wake her, as though she'd been drugged. He carries her out of the house and takes her back to his place where Mannie is waiting for him. Leaving Becky to take care of Teddy, the three men go to Jack's place. But the body is gone. In its place is a pile of thick gray fluff.

In the December 10 edition of *Collier's*, Miles and Jack wonder how many more duplicates are hidden away in secret places? Manny tells them not to worry. They have a mystery on their hands, he explains, but it's a completely normal mystery. Whose body was it and where is it now? Had they found the body before they knew about Santa Mira's strange epidemic, their imaginations wouldn't have run away with them. Teddy had seen what she expected to see, Jack's double. Just as Miles had seen Becky's double when, in fact, he'd seen nothing at all.

Miles returns to Becky's and finds only a mass of gray fluff where he'd seen her double. Disappointed but relieved, he accepts Manny's explanation. So does Becky. But Teddy isn't buying it and refuses to go home. Miles says she and Jack can stay at his place for a couple of days. Becky too!

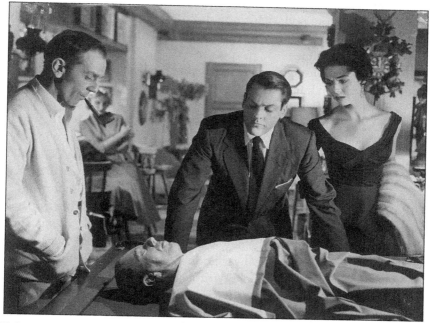

"It has all the features but no detail, no character, no lines," Miles notes. This is the second most often seen photograph from the film.

The next morning Jack shows Miles his collection of newspaper clippings, an assortment of odd events that were dismissed or ignored, but never explained. He picks one at random and gives it to Miles, a one-column item about a shower of frogs that fell on Alabama. The story was treated with humor, but no explanation was offered as to where the frogs had come from. Another clipping was an apology to a biology teacher named Bernard Budlong who denied having said that the mysterious seed pods found on a farm west of town were from outer space. Jack insists that just because a story can't be explained it shouldn't be dismissed. But just as Mannie had said they would, one by one the frightened patients return to Miles' office to say they've come to their senses. Everything's fine.

That evening Miles and Jack find four giant seed pods in Miles' cellar. Grayish heavy fluff spills out of the pods to form duplicates of each of them. Miles injects their doubles with air and they revert to gray fluff. He tries to phone for help but the operator won't put his calls through. The four of them hop into the car with the intention of going to the F.B.I. Before they've reached the city limits Miles notices that Becky has fallen asleep. Her face is pale and drained. He stops the car, opens the trunk, and finds two more pods, which he destroys. He sends Jack and Teddy to go for help. He and Becky return to Santa Mira to do what they can to thwart the invasion.

As they walk through town they realize how shabby it has become. They wonder when it happened. Gradually, they conclude, a little at a time.

When they see Wilma's car in front of Becky's house, they sneak up to one of the windows and listen to the conversation inside. They hear Wilma recalling her last conversation with Miles, repeating what she said to him with burlesque embarrassment. Uncle Ira, Aunt Aleda, and Becky's father all laugh. At that moment, Miles and Becky realize that these people are no longer human, but instead some alien life form.

Hoping to get to the bottom of the mystery, Miles and Becky pay a visit to the professor in Jack's newspaper clipping, Bernard Budlong. They ask him about the story in the newspaper. The professor explains that he was misquoted. During the conversation, Miles notices that the research material for a book the professor is writing is slightly faded and discolored. Like Santa Mira, it hasn't been attended to for a long time. Miles realizes the professor is a pod. He no longer has hope and ambition, which is why he'll never finish his book. The professor tells them with a shrug that he doesn't miss his emotions, and neither will they. He explains that the pods are parasites, drifting from planet to planet, duplicating whatever life form they find. But their lifespan is short. They're unstable, unable to hold form. Their life span is five years at the most. After that, the pods will move on, to search for life on some other planet.

As they leave the professor's house, Miles and Becky see Jack's car, speeding down the road, chased by the police. Jack had risked his own neck to let Miles know the police were after them. Becky and Miles realize there is no one they can trust.

In the final installment (December 24) Becky and Miles take refuge in his office, hoping that Jack managed to elude the police and that he will eventually bring help. Looking out the window, they see a horrible sight. The insidious pods are being distributed to the townspeople. The plan is clear: first Santa Mira, then all the towns around it.

Suddenly four men enter the office: Mannie Kaufman, Professor Budlong, and two other men. They intend to hold Miles and Becky prisoners until they fall asleep. They wait outside with a couple of pods, making Miles more determined than ever to remain human. He takes a male and female skeleton out of his closet and places them on the floor next to the door. He sprinkles them with blood and hair then loads four

Dana Wynter and Kevin McCarthy taking a break during the chase sequence in Bronson Canyon.

hypodermic syringes with morphine. He tapes two of the syringes to Becky's arms and two to his own. Miles hopes that the pods will duplicate the skeletons. When the skeletons collapse into dust he knows his plan has worked.

Manny and the others decide to keep Miles and Becky in jail until they've been duplicated. On the way down the stairs Miles and Becky use the hypos to kill their captors. They flee to the hills with no real hope of reaching the highway. They come upon a farm. In a thin line of irrigation ditches lay row after row of the horrible pods. In the barn next to the field, Miles finds six drums of gasoline. He and Becky pour the gas into the ditches and set fire to the pods.

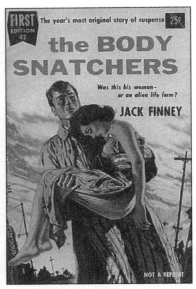

As they watch the burning field they are captured by the pod people. Then Jack shows up with the F.B.I. and the dead-eyed duplicates quietly drift back toward town. Suddenly the sky is peppered with dots as the pods leave a fierce and inhospitable planet. Miles is reminded of one of Churchill's war time speeches: "We shall fight them in the fields, and in the streets, we shall fight in the hills;

The cover of the Dell paperback.

we shall never surrender." The pods knew that. That's why they were leaving.

Jack Finney expanded his serial into a novel published as a paperback by Dell the following year. It had a slightly different ending. Once the pods return to the sky, the pod people drift back into town, leaving Miles and Becky behind. The Belicecs, who had been held prisoners, are waiting for them at their place. Within twenty minutes, the four of them are asleep. Miles tells the reader that none of the newspapers ever covered what happened in Santa Mira. It didn't even appear as a little one-column, tongue-in-cheek item that Jack Belicec would have added to his collection. But, Miles insists, showers of small frogs *do* fall from the sky and time is shifted and altered. You read the stories or hear vague rumors about these things and some of them are quite true.

CHAPTER TWO

HUNGRY FOR A HIT

There weren't many independent producers who could boast of having worked with so many major stars and directors on so many hit films as Walter Wanger. His name may not be as well known to the public as David O. Selznick or Sam Goldwyn, but Wanger stood right alongside them as one of Hollywood's most successful, independent filmmakers. He produced Frank Capra's *The Bitter Tea of General Yen* (1933), John Ford's *Stagecoach* (1939), Alfred Hitchcock's *Foreign Correspondent* (1940), and Fritz Lang's *Scarlet Street* (1945). He was responsible for the first outdoor Technicolor feature, *The Trail of the Lonesome Pine* (1936). At one time, he had more stars under contract that any other independent filmmaker. An intelligent, sophisticated maverick with a social conscience, he was given the National Peace Conference citation for his film *Blockade* (1938), the only movie to deal with the Spanish Civil War. The New York Theatre Arts Committee called him "The Movies' Man of the Year." Civic groups and social organizations sought his counsel and support. The Academy of Motion Picture Arts and Sciences gave him an honorary Academy Award in 1946 for his service as their president. Who would have ever guessed that ten years later he would be making a low budget science fiction movie at a poverty row studio?

Sadly, as it inevitably does to most people if they hang around long enough, Walter Wanger's magic touch turned into the Midas touch. It began with *Salome Where She Danced* in 1945. Although it gave a considerable boost to the career of actress Yvonne DeCarlo, the movie was pretty awful and didn't do anything for anyone else involved. After *Salome*, Wanger continued to produce pictures that nobody wanted to see. They weren't bad pictures. *Canyon Passage* (1946) was not only entertaining it was beautiful to look at. *The Lost Moment* and *Smash-Up; The Story of a Woman* (1947) were both solid pieces of entertainment, the latter earning Susan Hayward her first Oscar nomination. Unfortunately it's the box office returns, not the quality of a film, that dictates whether it's a success or not.

Poster from *Joan of Arc.*

Joan of Arc (1948) was the film that set the stage for Wanger's downfall. He was so sure the film would be a hit he sold the subsidiary rights to his entire film library to finance it. This explains why so many of his movies have fallen into the public domain. As anyone who has ever tried to track the ownership of an independently made film well knows, films are sold and re-sold, packaged and re-packaged so many times that, as often as not, the copyright is allowed to lapse because there isn't anyone to keep an eye on it. In some cases, the buyer may end up with a current copyright and nothing else because no one kept track of the negative or any of the other film elements. (As I write this, nobody seems to know who owns *The Body Snatchers*.)

Joan of Arc was a dream project for actress Ingrid Bergman. She'd played the role on Broadway and had been trying to get a screen version of Maxwell Anderson's play off the ground for years. She, Wanger, and director Victor Fleming formed Sierra Pictures to make it. They talked with MGM about releasing it, but in the end the studio backed out and the project ended up with the notorious Howard Hughes at RKO. It was a fortunate turn for Miss Bergman that Hughes decided to visit the set one afternoon. He saved her from what could have been a nasty spill. He happened to be near her when she fell off her horse. In the process of catching her, one of his hands ended up on her crotch. It was an awkward moment for them both.

Alas, *Joan of Arc* was not the screaming success that Wanger had hoped it would be. *Needed* it to be. There were those who pointed the finger of blame at Ingrid Bergman. Her illicit affair with Roberto Rossellini raised a lot of eyebrows at the time and supposedly it kept a lot of morally offended people away from the film. That, if you will forgive me, is a lot of baloney. The news of her affair broke long after *Joan of Arc* had come and gone.

Wanger said Howard Hughes was responsible for the film's failure, claiming the mogul hadn't promoted the picture. Frankly, that's a lot of baloney too. In one instance alone Hughes spent $75,000 to put an eight-story high figure of Ingrid Bergman in Times Square. Perhaps Wanger didn't agree with Hughes' brand of ballyhoo, but he couldn't, in all honesty, say that he hadn't tried.

Others blamed the 45 minutes that were cut from the picture when it went into general release, cuts that made the film somewhat confusing at times.

Officially, *Joan of Arc* was a flop. Supposedly, people stayed away in droves. That's not exactly true. It grossed six million bucks. That's a pretty hefty sum when you consider the average adult ticket price in those days was ninety cents. So people *did* come. They just didn't like what they saw. When the smoke cleared, the picture was still two million bucks in the hole.

Amazingly it won two Oscars and was nominated in six categories. Wanger was even given a special Academy Award for adding to the moral stature of the community. He refused it as a protest because the movie hadn't been nominated for best picture. In this writer's humble opinion, he was lucky to get what he got. *Joan of Arc* is not a very good picture and Ingrid Bergman is not very good in it. And for all of the money that was spent on the damn thing, it looks like one of those cheesy Universal-International sword and sandal movies. When Victor Fleming saw it, he was so depressed that he wept.

Wanger's next two pictures, both for the newly formed Eagle-Lion in 1949, were good ones. Making use of the sets from *Joan of Arc, Reign of Terror* was an exciting political thriller, directed by Anthony Mann and photographed by John Altman, two names that are well-known to fans of *film noir*. Unfortunately, it too was a failure. Changing the title to *The Black Book* didn't help it. But *Tulsa*, again with Susan Hayward, made some dough, which may have caused Wanger to believe that his run of bad luck had finally come to an end. He went heavily into debt to make *The Reckless Moment* (1949), a thriller about murder and blackmail starring his wife, Joan Bennett. It was based on Elizabeth Holding's novel *The Blank Wall*. When it failed to perform at the box office, it wasn't long before the bank was after Wanger to declare bankruptcy.

During this financial and artistic crisis, when it seemed as if things couldn't get any worse, they did. The beleaguered producer discovered that his wife, Joan Bennett, was having an affair with her agent, Jennings Lang. Many of their encounters were in the Beverly Hills apartment of one of Lang's subordinates. This was the inspiration a few years later for Billy Wilder's *The Apartment* (1960).

For Wanger it was the last straw. Having a reckless moment of his own, he confronted Lang in the parking lot at Universal Studios and shot him in the balls. Pleading temporary insanity to an attempted murder charge, Wanger spent four months in a prison honor camp. (There were many people who felt he should have been given a medal instead.) Emboldened or perhaps embarrassed, Wanger bragged to one reporter that while everyone in Hollywood complained about agents, he was the only one who'd ever done anything about them. Some people believed that when Wanger shot Lang, he was actually shooting all of the people who hadn't come to *Joan of Arc*.

The scandal made Wanger a laughingstock. When he got out of jail he found that Hollywood had turned its back on him. *Hey! Walt! Good to see you. Sorry I don't have time to talk to you.* The only door open to Wanger was at Monogram, a bottom of the barrel outfit best known for a series of East Side Kids movies. The producer spent the next two years grinding out a handful of fast-schedule, undistinguished potboilers that are best left forgotten. Where he'd once rubbed elbows with motion picture giants, it was beginning to look as if he would finish his career in the company such stalwarts as Leon Fromkess and Sigmund Neufeld.

It was Walter Mirisch who saved Wanger — though it was not his intention to do so. Mirisch was a producer at Monogram with some influence over the company's president, Steve Broidy. Mirisch convinced Broidy that it was time for the company to upgrade its image. As Monogram they could continue to mine their money-making Bowery Boys and Bomba franchises and then funnel some of that money into a new company, Allied Artists, which would make movies at a slightly higher level. Seeing a way out of the hole he was in, Wanger approached Broidy with an idea for a prison reform picture.

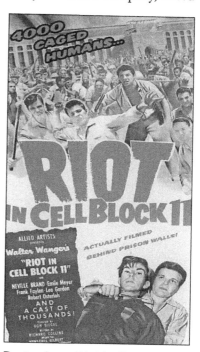

Riot in Cell Block 11 (1954) proved to be both a critical success and a big money-maker for Broidy's new company. It didn't put Wanger back in the big time but he was, at least, back in the game.

When Walter Wanger read the first installment of *The Body Snatchers* in Collier's, he immediately went after the screen rights. He later claimed that he felt the story had something important to say about the danger of conformity. That was something he cooked up after the fact. While you can build a case for that interpretation of Finney's story, you can't do it based on what's in that first install-

Poster from *Riot in Cell Block 11.*

ment. So it's safe to say that when Wanger approached Broidy with the idea of making Finney's serial into a movie back in November of 1954, he was pitching a science fiction thriller and nothing more.

Science fiction movies were growing in popularity at the time, especially with younger audiences. The major studios, for the most part, shied away from the genre, leaving it in the hands of the maverick filmmakers, working outside of the studio system, with incredibly low budgets. Edgar Ulmer's *The Man from Planet X* (1951), is one of the better examples of these early poverty offerings. It was shot in six days for under $50,000, on the sets left over from *Joan of Arc*.

Broidy had enjoyed some success with sci-fi — Walter Mirisch's *Flight to Mars* (1951) in Cinecolor, William Cameron Menzies' *The Maze* (1953) in

3-D, and Herman Cohen's *Target Earth!* (1954). So Broidy gave Wanger's project the green light. The budget was set at \$454,864 with a 24-day shoot. Finney was paid \$7500.

CHAPTER THREE

PREPRODUCTION

Walter Wanger chose Don Siegel to direct *The Body Snatchers*. Their experience together on *Riot in Cell Block 11* had been a good one. Siegel knew how to make a quality picture on a low budget. He'd learned a lot while he was working at Warner Brothers, first as the head of their montage department and later as an assistant director to Raoul Walsh and Michael Curtiz. Siegel knew where to put the lights and the camera and how to edit what he'd shot. He knew it all and he did it well. As far as Wanger was concerned, he was a godsend.

Siegel brought writer Daniel Geoffrey Holmes Mainwaring into the mix. Mainwaring had scripted Siegel's 1949 caper movie, *The Big Steal*, and the two men were friends. Mainwaring had also worked at Warner Brothers, as a publicist. He learned more about picture making from that job than he ever had as a novelist or a crime reporter. Like Wanger, he had a strong social conscience and shared Jack Finney's love for small town life. In some respects, he was the perfect man for the job.

The producer, the director, and the writer went to Mill Valley during the first week of the New Year to scout locations and to discuss the project with Jack Finney. Wanger immediately went to work developing background stories for the principal characters, which Mainwaring seems to have ignored. This is a shame. Wanger had some good ideas. If I were to lodge one complaint about the film (one that was shared by the film's star), it's the lack of flesh and blood characters. It's what keeps a really good movie from being a really great movie.

Wanger saw Miles Bennell as the kind of a guy who will always do the right thing in spite of the odds. He inherited his medical practice from his father and enjoys the fact that he knows everyone in town. He and his psychiatrist friend, Danny Kaufman, are working together to establish a medical research center that they both believe will greatly improve the health standards of Santa Mira. I think this would have been a nice touch. Miles and Danny could have talked about the center during their first scene in the parking lot. It would have cemented their close friendship and established them both as humanitarians and active members of the community. This kind of shading suggests that the characters actually had lives before the picture opened.

Dana Wynter played Becky Driscoll pretty much the way Wanger saw her — intelligent, wholesome and spirited. But Becky was one of those people who had little sympathy for people who couldn't make their marriages work and now that she's one of those people she isn't so sure of herself anymore. She's also embarrassed at having to move back in with her father. Her embarrassment and lack of confidence never made it to the script, so it's hardly surprising that it isn't part of Miss Wynter's performance.

Jack Belicec was a writer of mystery novels in the movie and in Finney's original, but Wanger saw him as another John Steinbeck, writing novels set in the area in which he lived. Unlike Steinbeck, however, Jack was not a raging success. Wanger may have wanted this change in the hope of injecting some of Steinbeck's outlook on life into the proceedings. Also (and this idea was not in Wanger's notes), if Jack wasn't successful, it would be easy for him to make a case for giving up after he became a pod.

The most interesting of all of the background stories is the one Wanger concocted for Jack's wife, Theodora. She was supposed to be the vision of the typical 1950s housewife, devoted and dependent on her husband with no life of her own. She loves having a writer for a husband and imagines that she is the heroine of his novels. She publicly supports Jack's disdain for organized religion, but is secretly religious. She also believes in ghosts and is emotionally unstable. None of this seems to have found its way into the script. While the character in the film does appear to be a little unstable, if not hysterical, her behavior isn't out of line. After all, she's way ahead of Jack and Miles. She *knows* the body is Jack's double.

Manfred Kaufman was supposed to be an oddball who bent over backwards to be a "regular" guy. He and Miles are best friends and have a mutual interest in each other's fields of medicine, although Miles doesn't share Manny's enthusiasm for hypnosis. Wanger counted on Manny's logical explanations for the strange events that take place in the story to steer the audience away from the truth.

Wanger's description of Miles' nurse, Sally Withers, makes me wish Mainwaring had taken some of the producer's suggestions to heart. "Full of bounce and the devil," he wrote, filling her nurse's costume to the best advantage, the dream of every male patient. Extremely capable and efficient, she and Miles engage in flirtations that would suggest they were having an affair though they are nothing more than friends.

Possibly with Siegel's help, Wanger made a list of the actors who could play these roles.

Miles Bennell: Richard Kiley, Eric Fleming, Darren McGavin, Lin McCarthy, John Baragray (yuck!), Charles Drake, Jack Kelly, MacDonald Carey, Joseph Cotton, Charlton Heston (ye Gods!), Robert Ryan, Philip Carey, Don Taylor, Barry Nelson, Ralph Meeker, Brian Keith, Steve Forrest, Jackie Cooper, George Nader and Kevin McCarthy.

Considered but crossed off the list: Richard Derr, James Daly, Richard Widmark, Van Heflin, Richard Basehart, Gig Young, and John Forsythe.

Becky Driscoll: Dana Wynter, Sally Brophy, Betsy Palmer, Elizabeth Montgomery, Joan Taylor, Joyce Holden, Maxine Cooper, Mary Sinclair, Allison Hayes (she would have been fun; she also could have played Sally only with more screen time), Delores Dorn, Nancy Olson, Barbara Hale, Kim Hunter, Joanne Dru, Donna Reed. (Dana Wynter heard that Vera Miles was in the running but she wasn't on the list.) I cast my vote for Myra Corday. She wasn't on the list, but that isn't my fault.

Considered, but crossed off the list: Lori Nelson, Ann Robinson, Janice Rule, Rhonda Fleming, Mona Freeman, June Haver, Vera Ellen, Dorothy Malone, Betsy Drake, Faith Domergue, Mary Murphy, Julie London (she would have been fun too).

Danny Kaufman: Larry Gates, Robert Cornthwaite, Anthony Ross, Robert Middleton, E.G. Marshall, Robert F. Simon, Arnold Moss, William Johnstone, James Gregory, John Newland, Walter Matthew, Robert Keith, Dean Jagger, Paul Stewart, Philip Ober, Henry Morgan, John Dehner, Whit Bissell, George Macready.

Jack Belicec: Rod Steiger, Cameron Mitchell, Bill Prince, Richard Boone, William Tallman, Hans Conried, Walter Matthew, James Gregory, Robert Cornthwaite, William Conrad, Lloyd Bridges, Joseph Wiseman, Murvyn Vye, Paul Richards, Sam Gilman, James Anderson, Richard Garland, Gene Wesson, Hugh Sanders, Earl Holliman, Hugh O'Brien, Hal Bokar.

Kevin McCarthy was the last name on the list of the actors considered for the role of Miles Bennell.

Theodora Belicec: Mercedes McCambridge, Claire Trevor, Audrey Totter, Julie Bishop, Virginia Field, Betsy Blair, Marie Windsor, Rita Johnson, Jeff Donnell, Helen Walker, Marsha Hunt, Cathy Lewis, Mary Anderson, Virginia Christine.

Sally Withers: Jean Willes, Joan Vohs, Martha Vickers, Helen Westcott, Helene Stanley, Nancy Gates (better as Becky), Virginia Gibson, Merry Anders.

Some of the people on Wanger's list, such as Richard Widmark and Charlton Heston, were probably just wishful thinking. Not only were these actors out of Wanger's price range, they were major stars, and major stars weren't in science fiction films at that time.

While Wanger and Siegel were in the process of casting the picture, Steve Broidy cut the budget to $350,000 and shaved four days off the schedule. A lot more names were crossed off the list. The lower budget also put the kibosh on filming in Mill Valley. Siegel had to find locations closer to home.

It may have been Siegel who recommended Kevin McCarthy for the lead. They'd recently worked together on another Allied Artists picture called *An Annapolis Story* (1954). The fact that McCarthy's name is the last one on the list suggests that he certainly wasn't Wanger's first choice.

McCarthy was living in New York at the time with his wife and three children, doing some radio and TV commercials to keep afloat, when he got the call from Siegel. The story that Siegel described sounded pretty far-fetched to McCarthy, but what the hell, it was a job. And for a change he'd be the star of the picture.

Dana Wynter you may have noted *was* at the top the list. By chance Wanger had seen her New York at the William Morris Agency. She had just signed with 20th Century-Fox. Wanger persuaded the studio to postpone the starting date of her contract so that she could be in his picture.

The rest of the cast:

Jack Belicec	King Donovan
Theodora "Teddy" Belicec	Carolyn Jones
Dr. Danny Kaufman	Larry Gates
Sally Withers	Jean Willes
Nick Grivett	Ralph Dumke
Wilma Lentz	Virginia Christine
Uncle Ira	Tom Fadden

Kevin McCarthy and Dana Wynter pose for art department stills.

Becky's father .... Kenneth Patterson
Sam Janzek ....Guy Way
Mrs. Grimaldi... Eileen Stevens
Grandma Grimaldi ....Beatrice Maude
Aunt Aleda .... Jean Andren
Jimmy Grimaldi ....Bobby Clark
Ed Pursey.. Everett Glass
Mac Lomax... Dabbs Greer
Baggage man...Pat O'Malley
Proprietor of the Sky View Terrace............................. Guy Rennie
Martha Lomax.. Marie Seland
Charlie Buckholtz .... Sam Peckinpah
Pod carrier... Harry J. Vejar.

Behind the camera:

Photographer .... Ellsworth Fredericks
Asst. Photographer..Phil Rand
Operator... Emmett Bergholz
Still Man ....Fred Morgan
Production design .... Edward "Ted" Haworth
Music..Carmen Dragon
Construction.. Jimmy West
Electrical..Ding Woodhouse
Production manager...Allen K. Wood
Production Secretary .... Phyllis Kerman
Assistant directors..Richard Maybery,
Bill Beaudine Jr. and Don Torpin
Film editor ....Robert S. Eisen
(though Richard Heermance actually oversaw the editing)
Sound .... Ralph Butler
Sound editor ....Del Harris
Boom Man .... Bob Quick
Grip..Harry Lewis
2nd Grip...Hilton Anderson
Prop...Elmer Stock
2nd Prop...Joe Yankol
Music editor .... Jerry Irvin
Set decorator ....Joseph Kish
Make-up .... Emile LaVigne

Hairdresser	Mary Westmoreland
Casting	Virginia Higgins
Casting Secretary	Midge Fisher
Wardrobe	Bert Kenrickson, Sid Mintz and Florence Hays
Gaffer	George Satterfield
Best Boy	Claire Sealey
Transportation	Cyril Poynton
Doorman	Charles Homberg
Laborer	Meyer Grace
First Aid	John Ward
Camera Equipment	Mark Armstead
Sound services	Lou Martin
Script supervisor	Irva Ross

Sam Peckinpah, the director of such noteworthy films as *Ride the High Country* (1962) and *The Wild Bunch* (1969), served as both dialog director and Don Siegel's personal assistant. His only credit on the film, however, is as an actor. Peckinpah often claimed that he wrote some of the picture, but he was talking through his hat.

Working closely with Siegel, Daniel Mainwaring finished the first draft of his screenplay on February 10. It was reasonably faithful to Jack Finney's serial, often incorporating much of his dialog. The script was forwarded to the Production Code office, headed by one Geoffrey M. Shurlock, for approval. While the basic story was acceptable to Mr. Shurlock, there were a few points of contention. What seemed to trouble him the most was the fact that the two lead characters had both been divorced. He couldn't see any reason for it and didn't think it would be any trouble to eliminate the few references to it. He also felt that it would be in the public interest to delete Danny Kaufman's line about shoving an ice pick into the base of a brain. To Shurlock's way of thinking it was a "bad detail of crime." And he wasn't happy with the exchange between Jack and Miles in the kitchen. Jack asks Miles if he and Teddy can stay for a while then, looking at Becky, adds "or did you have something else in mind?" Shurlock thought the line had an "objectionable sex suggestive quality."

Between the time that Mainwaring wrote the first and second drafts of the script, Dell paperbacks published the novelization of Jack Finney's serial. Mainwaring obviously read it for much of Finney's new dialog found its way into the seventy-five pages of his revisions, which were completed on March 2. He'd tightened the dialog from the previous draft, and changed the names of the Marin County towns that surrounded Santa Mira to fictitious ones. Somewhere along the way, Manny Kaufman became Danny Kaufman.

The third and final draft, completed on March 17, was forwarded to Mr. Shurlock. Again the watchdog of public morality urged them to remove all references to divorce. He noted that the use of the ice pick was still intact. So was that troublesome "sex suggestive" exchange in the kitchen.

And there were some additional problems.

Shurlock didn't want the stabbing of the duplicates with the pitchfork to be offensively gruesome. He thought the scene where Miles stabs the men with the hypodermic needles could be handled off-camera. And when it looks like Miles and Becky are going to have to join the pods and Becky says she'd rather die than live in a world without love or grief or beauty, Shurlock didn't care for Miles saying, "Not unless there's no other way." To him, it was an "unacceptable justification for suicide." Frankly, I can't imagine a better justification for suicide. Maybe Shurlock was a pod. What do you think?

None of the changes he asked for were made. His office had pretty much lost its grip on the motion picture industry. Censorship tends to exercise its greatest control over the most popular form of entertainment which was, by then, television. However, unless you were one of the major studios, and Allied Artists certainly wasn't, Shurlock's office could still make life miserable. Perhaps this was the reason for delaying Becky's introduction.

In the first two drafts of the script, Miles encounters Becky at the train station. He learns that she'd been on the train since Reno, where she'd gone for a divorce. In the final draft, she's introduced on page eight, when she comes to Miles' office to talk about Wilma, thereby postponing the conversation about their mutual divorces until page ten. This may have been an effort to appease Mr. Shurlock. Then again it may have simply been a desire to return the structure to the way Finney originally wrote it.

I want to put my two cents in here. Shurlock was wrong-headed about the divorce issue to say the least. Having two divorced characters that are willing to take another shot at matrimony is relevant to a story about a society that would give up everything important to avoid a little pain. But what would you expect from an agency that believed that the best way to deal with a problem was to pretend it didn't exist?

CHAPTER FOUR

SPECIAL EFFECTS

Don Siegel often bragged about how little they spent on special effects for *The Body Snatchers*, as if with his meager budget he had any choice. He went so far as to accuse other science fiction filmmakers of putting all of their money into special effects, at the sacrifice of everything else. One has to wonder who the devil he was talking about. Most of the 1950s science fiction movies were made for less than a third of the budget Siegel was working with and most of the special effects consisted of double exposures and whatever you could hang on a wire. More to the point, a faithful adaptation of Finney's serial would *never* have resulted in an effects-laden film. It simply wasn't that kind of a story.

There is only one special effects sequence in *The Body Snatchers* — the duplication of the four principals by the pods in the greenhouse. In Finney's story, the pods burst open in pieces like brittle leaves as the grayish substance inside pushes its way out. As the fluff spills into a puddle, the substance slowly turns white as it compresses itself into human form. When the process is completed the pods crumble to dust.

To do the duplication the way Finney described it would have required some expensive optical work, the kind that John Fulton did so well over at Paramount. Ted Haworth, the art director at Allied Artists, figured out a much cheaper way. He treated the duplication process like the birth of a baby. The pods split open in the middle and the duplicate pops out like a jack-in-the-box, covered with soap suds. Through cutting, the balloons are replaced by the body doubles created by the Don Post Studios.

Don Post was one of the first people to produce over-the-head Halloween masks for children. He and his crew made ten rubber pods for the greenhouse sequence and fifty cheaper plastic ones for all of the other scenes. The pods were sculpted out of clay from which casts were made. Liquid latex was used to make the "skins." The rubber pods were mounted on mechanized frames and were manipulated by hydraulics. Soap suds bubbled at the seams, the pods split open and compressed air forced the rubber human shapes to pop out.

The body molds of the four principals were supervised by Milt Rice. The actors were laid on slant boards to insure their muscles were in a natural position. Miss Wynter told Tom Weaver:

> I was in this [plaster cast] while it hardened and, of course it got rather warm! I was breathing through straws or something quite bizarre, and the rest of me was encased, it was like a sarcophagus.
>
> The guys who were making it tapped on the back of the thing and said, "Dana, listen, we won't be long, we're just off for lunch!"

Dave Allen, well-known to fans of stop-motion animation for his work on *When Dinosaurs Ruled the Earth* (1970) and *Caveman* (1981), bought foam rubber from Don Post to make his early stop motion puppets. One afternoon he took me with him to the studio. Neither of us knew that Post had worked on *The Body Snatchers* until we saw the photograph on the wall of Dana Wynter, standing beside the cast that was made from her body.

"Did you make the pods too?" I asked Post.

"Oh sure," he said. "We made a bunch of 'em. We did a couple of those science fiction pictures. We worked on one called *Space Master X-7*. That one was real easy. We just threw a bunch of latex rubber on the floor and let it dry."

Earlier that year I'd called Allied Artists in the hope of getting my hands on one of the pods. I thought that maybe, just maybe, they might have one lying around in some dark corner that they might be willing to part with. The operator put me through to one of the sound stages and I found myself talking to Ted Haworth. He said they'd just gotten rid of the last one a couple of weeks ago.

"I don't know why you'd want one of those things anyway," he said. "That movie wasn't so hot."

Idiot!

Now I was standing next to the man who had actually made the pods. My hope of finally securing one was at an all time high. I asked Mr. Post if, by chance, he'd kept any of the pods. Before he could answer he launched into a horrible, gut-wrenching coughing fit, the likes of which I'd never seen. This jag was the result of breathing all of those toxic fumes from the chemicals that he worked with. Had he fallen down dead right then

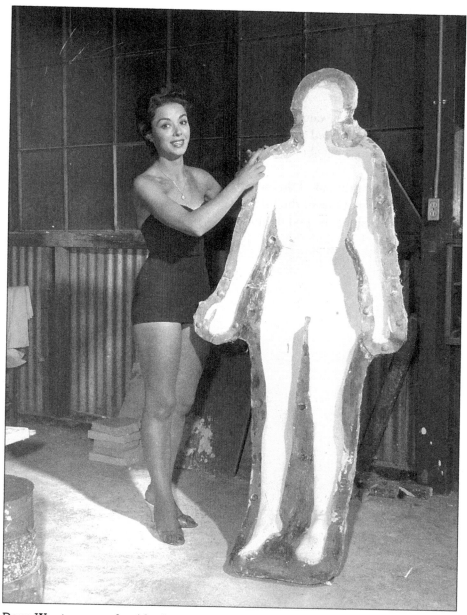

Dana Wynter poses beside the cast made of her body at Don Post Studios.

and there I would have been shocked, but not surprised. Dave told me later that this happened often which explained why he didn't seem the least bit concerned at the time.

I can't say how long it took Mr. Post to recover. It seemed like forever. But after keeping me in suspense, he finally got control of himself and gave me an answer.

"Nope."

Don Siegel was waiting for Kevin McCarthy when his TWA flight from New York landed at the airport.

"Well, kiddo, what about it? Do you think we can pull this off?" Siegel asked.

McCarthy grinned. "I do indeed."

I imagine that one of the first things on the agenda was a trip to Don Post Studios since the pod doubles had to be ready to go when the filming began.

CHAPTER FIVE

MAKING THE MOVIE

On March 23, 1955, shooting began on Allied Artists production number 5504. Trucks and busses began rolling out of the studio lot at six a.m. Destination: Sierra Madre. Siegel had twenty days to make the movie. He took twenty-three.

The stated reason for the picture going over schedule was Siegel's insistence on shooting night-for-night scenes. I don't believe it. Of course this is only a supposition on my part you understand, but I don't think Siegel ever intended to finish the picture on schedule. Broidy had originally given Walter Wanger twenty-four days and I think the director wanted some those days back. The extra time threw the picture $82,190 over budget. That's pretty small potatoes in the grand scheme of things.

1ST DAY: SCENES 15B, 15C, 105-108, AND 262

The very first scene photographed was the farmers loading pods onto their truck from Miles' point of view. The location was at the Goya Nursery at 600 Wilcox Street in Sierra Madre. The nursery and the street no longer exist. Its owner, Paul Goya, moved to Arizona where he continued his farming skills at the Gila River Relocation Center.

Sierra Madre is a sleepy little bedroom community in the foothills of the San Gabriel Mountains, west of Arcadia (the city where I grew up) and east of Pasadena. Sierra Madre Boulevard, the next stop for Siegel, was the town's main street which had been blocked off. Santa Mira had been painted over all of the Sierra Madre signs.

The exterior of Dr. Bennell's office was a business building on the south side of Sierra Madre Boulevard. The back of the building once housed The Sierra Madre Hotel. That morning they filmed the scene where Miles and Becky step out of that building, have a brief encounter with Sam Janzek, and then cross the street to the hardware store that Becky's father owns.

The next set-up was a block away on the south corner of Sierra Madre Boulevard and Baldwin Avenue — Wilma Lentz's Antique Store. They shot the exterior and interior of the store. The building is no longer there. In its stead is a parking lot for the local market.

2ND DAY: SCENES 14, 180, 184, 186, 188, 190, 192, 194, 227-230 AND 233

Again on Sierra Madre Boulevard, Miles and Becky attempt to escape from Santa Mira by posing as pod people. Their effort is thwarted when Becky cries out as a dog is about to be hit by a truck. Her emotional outburst causes Officer Sam Janzek to become suspicious. He goes to Miles office to make sure everything is on the up and up.

The next thing on the agenda was the distribution of the pods to the Santa Mira residents, witnessed by Miles and Becky from his office window. This took place in the triangular square located at Sierra Madre

Wilma Lentz (Virginia Christine) drops the pretense of being human as she enters her antique store.

Boulevard, Baldwin Avenue, and Kersting Court. Local residents were recruited for this sequence. In fact, the schools closed early that day. You can see a couple of children in the scene.

Later, some of these same people were told to run through the streets. They didn't know who or what they were supposed to be running from, but it didn't matter. They were in a movie! These scenes were shot exclusively for the trailer. They do not appear in the film.

The Body Snatchers may have been the biggest thing that ever happened to Sierra Madre. The residents have all but forgotten that Bob Hope was once there to film *The Seven Little Foys* (1955). And though there have been half a dozen movies shot there since, it was the two days that Siegel and his crew showed up that left the greatest impression. The film has become part of the town's culture. Every now and then it celebrates something called "Pod Day," though I have no idea what they do in this celebration. (I know. I know. I should.) Maybe it's because the Bob Hope film restricted its filming to a single home. Maybe it's because the residents got to play a part in the film. Maybe it's because *The Body Snatchers* is the most famous of the movies that have been shot there.

One of my favorite stories about the effect that the movie had on the town comes from the book *"They're Here..."* which is a tribute to the film. One of the residents, angry at the city council for making what he felt were stupid decisions, went to the trouble of making a papier-mâché pod for each member of the council, with their picture and name on it. The pods were left in the middle of Kersting Court.

While Siegel and his crew were busy in Sierra Madre, Walter Wanger hired Richard Collins to do some fast re-writes. Collins had scripted *Riot in Cell Block 11* and another Wanger film, The *Adventures of Hajji Baba* (1954). Collins was one of the many writers who had been blacklisted when the House on Un-American Activities Committee blew through Hollywood looking for communists. He refused to testify when he was first called before the committee and lost his job at Warner Brothers because of it. After four years of unemployment, Collins agreed to become a "friendly" witness. He gave the committee the names of twenty-six former communist party members, his own wife, Dorothy Comingore, among them. She was called before the committee and refused to do what her husband had done. Collins divorced her and took the kids.

Why Daniel Mainwaring wasn't asked to do these re-writes is anybody's guess. It's possible that he wasn't available. It's also possible that ıs would have been Wanger's choice to script the picture from the o had it not been for Siegel. Whatever, the sequences that Collins ...— ı hand in are all in the first half of the script. I suspect that he did little more than tighten the dialog. Whatever his participation was it wasn't enough to warrant a screen credit.

3RD DAY: SCENES 21-26

The house used for the Lentz home was across the street from a Glendale park at 1635 Rancho Avenue. According to the press book, the owner was paid to let his lawn grow so that Uncle Ira would have something to mow while Miles is talking to Wilma Lentz. Pressbooks are notoriously reckless with the truth but this story, however uninteresting, sound plausible.

4TH DAY: SCENES 3A-6, 8-10

On location in Chatsworth to film the train depot and Grimaldi's vegetable stand. The depot is no longer there. It was located west of the train tracks, north of Dupont Street and east of Remmet Avenue, due west and north of the current Chatsworth Metrolink Station near the intersection of Mayall Street and Old Depot Plaza Road. The dirt road seen on the process screen when Miles is driving away from the station was west of the depot, paralleling the train tracks. Grimaldi's Vegetable Stand was located near the intersection of Mason Avenue and Lassen Street.

5TH DAY: SCENES 232, 234-250

Beachwood Village is a town even smaller than Sierra Madre, nestled in the hills below the famous Hollywood sign in Beachwood Canyon. The chase begins when Miles and Becky race past the Richfield Station at the junction of Beachwood Drive, Belden Drive, and Westshire Drive. They continue up Westshire Drive to what Kevin McCarthy described as "those long, interminable stairs."

The crew rigged a gizmo out of block and tackle so the camera could dolly back, looking down on Kevin and Dana as they ran up the stairs. A less dedicated director would never have gone to so much trouble. There were lots of ways Siegel could have filmed this shot. He chose the one that was the most difficult and the most effective.

At the top of the stairs (after the lunch break) Miles and Becky ran across Hollyridge Drive, down the hillside to Bronson Canyon and the cave, located at the north end of Canyon Drive.

6TH DAY: SCENES 253, 256-259A&B, 261, 264-280

The entire day was spent in and around Bronson Canyon Caves, one of Hollywood's most often used locations. If you're any kind of film fan, you're as familiar with it as your own backyard. It was once the site of a quarry, founded by the Union Rock Company in 1903 for the excavation of crushed rock. As soon as the Union Rock Company moved out the film crews moved in. The location was a favorite of 1950s sci-fi films. *Atom Man vs. Superman, Mark of the Gorilla* (1950), *Unknown World* (1951), *Robot Monster* (1953), *The Snow Creature, Killers from Space* (1954), *King Dinosaur* (1955), *The Day the World Ended, It Conquered the World, Man Beast* (1956), *The Cyclops, The Brain from Planet Arous, Attack of the Crab Monsters* (1957), *Night of the Blood Beast, Earth vs. The Spider, Monster from Green Hell, The Return of Dracula, Viking Women and the Sea Serpent, Teenage Caveman, She Demons* (1958), *Invisible Invaders, The Cosmic Man, Have Rocket, Will Travel* and *Teenagers from Outer Space* (1959) all used Bronson Canyon. And those are just the ones that I can remember.

The pod people are in pursuit of Miles and Becky. Several of the people in this still were used on some of the posters.

Everything inside and outside of the cave had to be shot in one day. Neil Rau, a reporter for *The Los Angeles Examiner* was on hand to cover the scene where Miles and Becky fall in the mud and Miles discovers that she's become a pod. Rau, once a legman for Louella Parsons, reported that he found the couple pitching "goo" instead of woo. "Just call me muddy Lancaster," McCarthy told him with a grin, a reference to the famous love scene in *From Here to Eternity* (1953). Don Siegel said he was getting a lot of satisfaction out of the scene because the censors couldn't clean it up no matter how hard they tried. "And what about Dana," Siegel added, "is she the poor man's Esther Williams with mud in her eye?" Rau thought Dana, even with a mud pack, was as beautiful as she had been reported to be. "They say the Italians go in for realism," she told Rau. "Well, they can't beat us."

I would be remiss in my duty if I didn't say that these quotes sound like the invention of a desperate writer trying to punch up a pretty dull article. Writers make up stuff all of the time and nobody cares because (at least in this case) it's harmless. And, after all, publicity is publicity. And this was a film that needed all of the publicity that it could get.

Dana Wynter said Kevin McCarthy had the good manners not to mention the fact that she was a little heavy when they filmed this scene.

Kevin McCarthy and Dana Wynter in Bronson Caves.

For my money, one of the best shots in *The Body Snatchers* is the moment when Miles and Becky have crawled into a ditch inside of the tunnel to hide beneath some planks. We see the pod people rushing toward the entrance as Miles puts the last plank in place. It wasn't an easy shot to get because of the contrast between the darkness inside of the cave and the sunlight outside. It was Siegel's intention to hold on the shot long enough for several people to run over the planks and past the camera. Officer Janzek is the first one to enter the tunnel. He pauses for a moment, barks some orders, and runs off. And that's when one of the extras tripped and fell. There wasn't time for a second take. The editor held on the shot for as long as he possibly could, a little too long, in fact, for if you look closely you can see the guy start to fall. A few more frames and you would have seen him kiss the plank.

7TH DAY: SCENES 52-54, 66-68, 70, 75-82

After what had been an exhausting two days, the two leads had the next day to relax a little. They weren't on call until that evening when they

Kevin McCarthy and Dana Wynter in Bronson Caves.

shot all of the scenes inside and outside of the Driscoll house, located at 1927 Rodney Drive in Hollywood. Most of the houses on the block, including the one used for the movie, have been replaced by apartments.

8TH DAY: SCENES 157-165

This was another night shoot, this time at Sally's house at 4400 Russell Street in Los Angeles. (It's still there.) Miles and Becky stop at the curb. Miles goes to the window of the house and sees the pod people inside, slugs the cop, and races back to the car with the pod people on his heels.

9TH DAY: SCENES 142-143, 145, 146, 181, 183, 187, 189, 191, 193, 195-199

This was the first day at the Allied Artists studio, located at 4401 West Sunset Boulevard in Los Angeles. When Allied Artists stopped making movies in the sixties, the studio was sold to KCET, a public television station. Huell Howser probably did a show about it.

Extras wait for Don Siegel to call for action so they can resume the chase.

What they filmed on this day were the scenes of Miles and Becky watching the distribution of the pods from the office window and the arrival of Jack and Danny as pod people. The hypodermic scene was saved for the next day.

That night they went to the gas station (no longer there) at 1200 N. Virgil Avenue, on the corner of Virgil Avenue and Lexington Avenue. Miles pulls into the station to get some gas and make a phone call. He sees the gas jockey messing with the trunk of his car. When Miles drives off he goes down Virgil Avenue, turns west onto Lexington Avenue and into an alley halfway down the street where he stops just long enough to take the pods out of his trunk and burn them.

10TH DAY: SCENES 41, 42, 42A, 200-206

In the script, while Jack and Danny are waiting for Miles and Becky to fall asleep, they're sitting in Miles' reception room watching the pods grow. (Siegel had intended to show the duplicates forming but somewhere along the line he changed his mind about that; there probably wasn't time for

Held captive in his own office, Miles and Becky learn about the origin of the pods.

Kevin McCarthy and Larry Gates take a break between scenes.

it.) When they hear the shattering of glass in the other room they rush out to see what's going on. They find Becky slumped in a chair. Miles is at the medicine cabinet with a hypodermic in his hand. Danny asks Miles what he's doing. Miles says he's putting himself to sleep. Danny tells him that he mustn't do that. (I guess we're supposed to assume that a drugged mind will jeopardize the duplication process.) Jack lifts Becky out of the chair and shakes her. As she slumps forward against him, she jabs him in the stomach with a hypodermic full of morphine. Miles stabs Danny in the neck then quickly refills the hypo. He flattens himself against the wall and Becky jerks the door open. Nick Grivett, who has been trying to bust the door down, rushes in, and Miles stabs him in the neck. This is similar to but not quite the way the scene plays itself out in the film. Siegel changed it on the set.

That night they filmed the scene where Miles and Becky arrive at Jack's house. The location was on a five acre estate owned by newspaper publisher Harry Chandler in the Los Feliz section of Los Angeles.

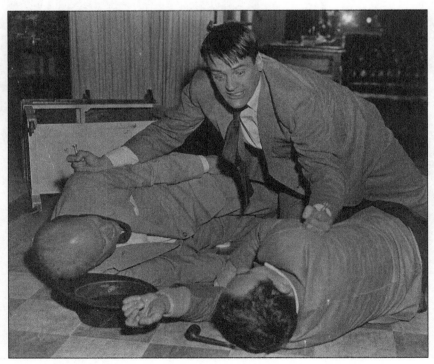

This is a specially posed photograph. In the film Kevin McCarthy has already plunged the hypos into Larry Gates and King Donovan before the three men hit the floor. Note that Larry Gates (bottom left) is smiling.

Chandler's massive two-story brick mansion wasn't used. Jack Belicec would have had to have been one helluva writer to afford something like that. Instead, they used the guest house. At the time there was a front entrance to the property at 2330 Hillhurst Avenue and a back entrance at 2411 Inverness Avenue. When the property was subdivided, only the back entrance remained.

11TH DAY: SCENES 15A, 170, 171, 174, 207, 225, 226, 231

Speaking of subdivisions, I have to point out that there were three locations for Dr. Bennell's office. As previously stated, the interior of the office was an Allied Artists set. The front of the building was in Sierra Madre. The hallway and stairs, front and back, belonged to a medical building at 1710 N. Vermont Avenue in Los Angeles, on the east side of the street, between Kingswell Avenue and Prospect Avenue. The used car lot where Miles and Becky leave their car was just a parking lot in the rear of the building. While both buildings have similar double doors at their entrances, the glass above the door in Sierra Madre is round and divided

Miles searches for Becky's double in the Driscoll cellar.

like a pie. The window above the door on the Los Angeles building is square with no dividers. (This is butt-crack at its finest.)

On this day, they filmed all of the scenes in the hallway and the stairs, the outside back stairs, and the used car lot.

12TH DAY: SCENES 284-290

The climax of the film took place on the Mulholland Drive bridge over the Hollywood Freeway. It took them all night to shoot it.

"We rented about fifty cars and crossed our fingers," Siegel told me. "We shot the last scene just before dawn."

To make the sequence as believable as possible, Siegel avoided the use of any trick camera work and there was never a double for Kevin McCarthy. There were stuntmen in the cars nearest to him. At one point McCarthy was so exhausted Siegel was afraid his timing would be off and he'd end up under the wheels of one of the cars.

13TH DAY: SCENES 71-74

Kevin McCarthy was the only actor on call this day. They only shot his search of the cellar in the Driscoll home, which was a set on the Allied Artists lot. It couldn't (or shouldn't) have taken long. I suspect everyone needed a break after working all night on what must have been a difficult sequence.

14TH DAY: (29-39)

The last day of location shooting was reserved for all of the scenes pertaining to The Sky Terrace Nightclub (listed on the location sheet as The Fireside Inn) at the San Fernando Valley Country Club in Woodland Hills at 21150 Dumetz Road. It was one of Siegel's concessions to shooting day-for-night.

15TH DAY: SCENES 43-51

Siegel spent the day on the sequence surrounding the body on Jack's pool table. He did everything up to the point where Jack cuts his hand.

16TH DAY: SCENES 55-57, 60

Again at Jack's house, Teddy sees that the body has changed into Jack. Jack and Miles and Danny return only to discover that the body is gone. All of the scenes in Miles' living room were filmed as well.

17TH DAY: SCENES 99-103

They shot the sequence in Miles' kitchen that so troubled Mr. Shurlock.

18TH DAY: SCENES 115-137
Considering the amount of dialog, the number of camera angles, and the mechanical effects involved in the greenhouse sequence, it's amazing that Siegel was able to complete it in a single day.

19TH DAY: SCENES 64A, 250, 252, 278
Siegel shot the scene of Miles running out of his back door to rescue Becky, the scenes of Miles and Becky hiding beneath the planks, and a close up of Miles shouting directly into the camera (supposedly on the freeway overpass).

20TH DAY: SCENES 7, 8, 11, 27A, 154, 160
These were all of the scenes inside of Miles' car against a process screen.

21ST AND 22ND DAY: SCENES 12-15, 16-20, 177-179
Back to Miles' office for the discussion between Miles and Sally about the cancelled appointments; Becky's introduction; Jimmy Grimaldi arrival

Dana Wynter, Carolyn Jones, Kevin McCarthy, and King Donovan watch in horror as they are being duplicated by the seed pods.

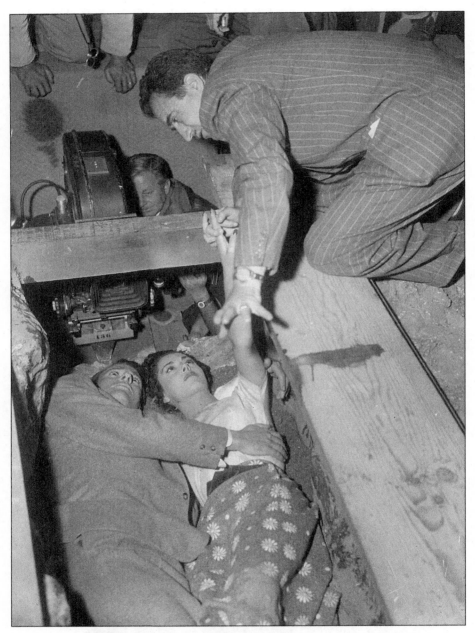

At the studio, Kevin McCarthy and Dana Wynter get instructions from Don Siegel. That's Ellsworth Fredericks behind the camera.

with his grandmother; Miles and Becky hiding in the closet; their observation about people's loss of humanity, and the two of them waiting for Jack to arrive with help the next morning.

23RD DAY: SCENES 86-98

On April 18, the final day of shooting, they were in Becky's basement once again with Danny trying to convince Miles and Jack that their imaginations were running away with them. After that, they finished the pool table sequence.

Kevin McCarthy, Dana Wynter, and Carolyn Jones were back at the studio the following day for a photo shoot. These were specially posed stills for the posters. Had Allied Artists decided to use artwork instead photographs for the posters these stills would have been used as reference for artists.

CHAPTER SIX

LOOKING FOR ORSON WELLES

It is no secret that Don Siegel hated the new opening and closing that was imposed on the picture by the studio executives. He fought it tooth and nail, but it was one of the many battles he lost.

When Steve Broidy and Harold Mirisch saw the rough cut of the picture they liked it but they thought the ending was too abrupt and too downbeat. It wasn't until they saw it with an audience that they panicked and insisted on the changes that Siegel hated so much. The two executives, Broidy more so than Mirisch, have always been painted as the villains of the story. Siegel referred to them as pods. Kevin McCarthy called them the pod police. But in a conversation I had with McCarthy, he implied that Walter Wanger was partly to blame for what happened to the film. McCarthy thought Wanger was a little weak in the knees when it came to dealing with the front office. After looking through the files, I have come to the conclusion that he may have been right.

I don't want to be too hard on Walter Wanger. From all accounts he was a good man and a good, supportive producer. However, at this stage of his career, I think he was also a very frightened man. On one hand he wanted (and needed) to make a commercial success but on the other hand he wanted to make an "important" picture, the kind of a picture that would get him back into major film production. It was Wanger, not Broidy or Mirisch, who was afraid that the audience wouldn't understand his picture. He was the one who thought they might not be able to follow the story even though he'd always said you should never underestimate the intelligence of the audience. Long before Broidy demanded the frame story, Wanger was writing narration to open the picture. The frame story opened the door to have narration running throughout the picture. I can't see why Wanger would have been against it. Narration could highlight the subtleties that he thought the viewer might miss and at the same time remind them of what they'd already seen. According to the files, Broidy only asked for the bookends. He didn't ask for narration. The fact that Wanger was tampering with the movie before Siegel had finished shooting it, long before anybody had said anything about changing anything, strongly suggests he was the one who wanted it.

On the 28th of March, Wanger wrote to an Allied Artists executive in England about using a quotation from a speech that Winston Churchill had recently made to the House of Commons: "The day may dawn when fair play, love for one's fellow men, respect for justice and freedom, will enable tormented generations to march forth serene and triumphant from the hideous epoch in which we have to dwell. Meanwhile, *never flinch, never weary, never despair.*"

Make of that what you will. Exactly what that has to do with seed pods, I really couldn't say. But if Wanger thought a quote from Churchill would add a note of respectability to his film he might just as well have lifted the one Jack Finney used in his serial. It was a better fit.

At the beginning of May, Wanger wrote some narration to open the film. Miles Bennell introduces himself: an ordinary guy living an ordinary life. That is, until the day he's going to tell us about — a day that began like any other day until he put a few pieces together and realized that the world was facing a threat more terrible than the atomic bomb.

Unsatisfied with his new opening, even after Richard Collins had polished it, Wanger wrote another one that was almost identical to the way Jack Finney opened his novel. It was sent to Kevin McCarthy. Its purpose, the actor was told, was to prepare the audience for the exciting, impossible, strange, and horrible things that were going to follow. Why would Wanger think they needed to be prepared? It harkens back to the early days of sound movies, when actor Edward Van Sloan appeared before the credits of *Frankenstein* (1931) to warn the audience they were about to see something that might frighten them.

One of the things I like best about *The Body Snatchers* is the way it creeps up on you. Apparently Wanger didn't want it to creep. He wanted it to pounce.

In the movie, after Miles gets off the train, he almost runs over a little boy, Jimmy Grimaldi. The child is running away from his mother, Anna, because he knows she's an imposter. Miles has a brief conversation with the woman then returns to his car. His nurse tells him that Anna had been in to see him while he was away at the convention but since the woman made no mention of it during her brief exchange with Miles he assumes it couldn't have been anything serious. Wanger thought this was too light, too subtle. Hoping that Allied Artists would spring for some retakes, he wrote some new dialog for the nurse.

"Don't think I'm crazy Doc," Sally tells Miles, "and if you do, send me away because I can't stand it here in Santa Mira anymore." She knows that something terrible is happening but she can't quite put her finger on it. But things aren't right. She's sure of that much and Miles shouldn't let anyone convince him otherwise.

Let's examine this piece of business, because I think it's important. If Sally felt this way wouldn't it have been the first thing she said to Miles when she met him at the station? And why would she need Miles to send her away if she felt like going? Furthermore, why would Wanger think he could have her say something like this and not write something for Miles to say in response? No matter. By adding narration, Wanger was able to alert the audience to the potential danger without adding a new scene. Miles tells the audience that the boy's panic should have told him it was more than school he was afraid of; the littered, closed up vegetable stand should have told him something too.

Much later in the story, when Miles and Becky are told by Danny Kaufman that they have to become pod people, Wanger wanted to flesh out Danny's dialog with an additional scene. He wanted the psychiatrist to reinforce the idea that their fate was sealed. There was nothing they could do to turn the tide and that somehow it was their fault. They'd waited until the last minute. They'd waited until it was too late. "We've brought it on ourselves," he tells them. We've subverted ourselves. We can't escape it. *They're* taking over.

Along these same lines, Wanger wrote a bit of dialog for one of the pod people. As Miles races toward the highway to warn people of the threat in Santa Mira, one of the pod people says, "I told you he was dangerous to us. He won't give up. Someone will listen to him. One honest man can ruin us. That's how we have always been beaten."

One *honest* man can ruin us. What the devil is Wanger getting at? More important, who else has beaten the pod people? Other life forms on other planets? And if they've *always* been beaten it wouldn't seem as if they pose much of a threat.

Both of these additions, the one for the pod man and the one for Danny Kaufman, sound like something out of one of Wanger's earlier political thrillers. They simply don't fit here. We can all be thankful that Broidy didn't spring for those retakes.

There is a brief moment in the film in Wilma's Antique Shop where Wilma blandly says to Becky's father, "Becky's still at his house." To which he blandly replies, "All right." It suggests some kind of a conspiracy between them. As the film unravels we discover that the whole town is involved in a conspiracy. Wanger wanted to stress this aspect of the story. Again he was afraid that the audience wouldn't get it.

In the film, after Miles drives away from the gas station with two pods in the trunk of his car, Wanger wanted the gas station attendant to call the chief of police. "We've got everything covered," the chief assures him. "There are road blocks out."

Wanger also wanted to stress how ruthless the pod people could be. To that end he wrote (or had someone write) a brief sequence in which Jack and Teddy encounter one of these roadblocks. Jack hits the brakes. His car skids into a ditch. He tells Teddy to run for it and hurls himself at the two policemen. During the struggle, he's knocked out. While one of the cops stands guard, the other hops into the patrol car to chase after Teddy. He runs her down and tosses her body into a ditch.

After Sam Janzek sees the bodies of the three men in Miles' office, he gets on his police radio and says, "This is Janzek. They got away. Turn the main siren on." Wanger wasn't sure the audience would understand that it was a life or death situation for Miles and Becky. He wanted Janzek to say: "They killed the Chief and Dr. Kaufman, and Jack. Everybody must get out on a manhunt to get 'em and shoot to kill. They mustn't get away."

If the audience didn't understand that Miles and Becky were in jeopardy at this stage of the game, it's doubtful that any line of dialogue would have helped.

Wanger wasn't satisfied with the scene where Becky changes into a pod. No, he wasn't worried about the fact that her transformation takes place faster than we've been told was possible. He wanted to somehow instill the feeling in the audience that this event had intensified Miles' resolve to warn the world about what was happening in Santa Mira. He didn't want it to appear that Miles was simply running away from a bad situation.

Had Wanger had his way, I dare say his changes would have caused far more damage to the film than the frame story ever could have.

In his quest to make an "important" film, Walter Wanger sought the aid of Orson Welles. Why Welles? I don't know. I guess if you believed that having a quote from Winston Churchill would add prestige to your film, it stands to reason that actually *having* someone famous would be even better.

In June, after consulting with Steve Broidy, Wanger began negotiations with Welles' agent, Lee Katz. The plan was to have Welles open and close his film and do the trailers and TV spots as well.

Wanger's new opening begins on the highway, just off Highway 101 where it supposedly intersects the road to Santa Mira. Sirens roar and traffic is wild. A truck is parked on a dirt road and the operator is looking anxiously around with a microphone in his hand. Orson Welles dramatically appears, running out of the darkness to take the microphone. He tells his radio audience that he's just outside "the town on which the eyes of the whole world are focused tonight." He's just heard a strange and most frightening story from a man named Dr. Miles Bennell who some people think is mad. Welles is convinced that he's telling the truth.

Welles returns at the conclusion of the story to say how lucky we are that someone finally listened to Dr. Bennell. "Let's hope that what went on here will stand as an object lesson to every human man," he concludes. "In this day and age anything can happen and if you're asleep when it does, you're next!"

Believe it or not, even after Mainwaring's frame story had been written, Wanger was still hot on the idea of having Orson Welles open and close the film. So he incorporated Mainwaring's frame story into a new script for Welles, effectively making it a wraparound of a wraparound. This time Welles is sitting in his study, looking at the front page of a newspaper. He introduces himself, talks about his radio broadcast of *War of the Worlds* and how surprised he was at the panic it caused. Now he understands why it did. The supersonic age, the atomic age, has made it seem as if anything is possible. Men fly faster than the speed of sound. Space travel and space stations are but a few years off. For all we know, shooting stars could be flying saucers. Each day seems to bring something new to chill our spines. Like what's been happening in Santa Mira. At this point Mainwaring's frame story begins. Welles invites the audience to be the judge as to whether the story it's about to hear is unbelievable or not.

At the conclusion, we return to Welles who gets out of his chair, lights a cigarette and comes toward the camera. He asks if we were to encounter a man in the night with a story that sounded crazy, would we listen? We'd better. Because anything can happen in this day and age, and if it does he says, pointing his finger at the camera, "You're next!"

Fortunately, getting a straight answer from the elusive Mr. Welles proved to be quite a challenge for Wanger. Welles was running all over Europe at the time, playing hide and seek with his agent. When Katz was finally able to pin him down Welles expressed as little interest in the project as he possibly could without actually turning it down. He wanted more money, of course. And he wanted to re-write and direct the thing himself. In a letter to Walter Mirisch, Lee Katz assured him that Welles would have his way. No director could control him. And it was no secret that Welles liked to ham it up. At one of his recent stage performances, Katz said little of the scenery was left unchewed.

Between Welles' unreasonable demands and the inability of his agent to pin him down, the deal fell through. Wanger went looking for someone else.

Edward R. Murrow, a broadcast journalist well-known for his honesty and integrity, and one of the only people to challenge Senator Joseph McCarthy's communist witch hunt, looked good to Wanger. They could use Murrow's *Person to Person* television format to make it appear as if Murrow had been following the Santa Mira mystery all along and was finally getting the opportunity to interview Miles Bennell. At the conclusion of the story, Murrow would thank Dr. Bennell and say something to the effect that so long as people believed in faith, decency, and the dignity of man, the world would be safe.

In the event that Murrow didn't pan out, Wanger had two other respected journalists in mind: Lowell Thomas and Quentin Reynolds. Ray Bradbury, the famous science fiction author, was also in the running.

Eventually Wanger gave up on the idea because he wanted to finish the picture in time for a festival in Edinburgh. He thought, and rightly so, that a little international publicity would help promote the picture. I don't know if the picture ever made it to that festival, but I'm glad the whole idea of having a celebrity open the picture never saw the light of day. This is the sort of ballyhoo better suited to a William Castle movie. Having Welles or anyone else introduce the picture wouldn't have made it any better and more than likely would have cheapened it.

As a possible minor note of interest, there *was* a producer who was able to get Orson Welles to huckster a science fiction picture. Welles narrated the trailers for producer Albert Zugsmith's *The Incredible Shrinking Man* in 1957. Welles was directing a movie for Zugsmith at the time. That probably had something to do with it.

Allied Artists was not in the habit of holding sneak previews of their movies, but Wanger insisted on getting an audience reaction to his film.

There were three sneak previews of *The Body Snatchers* on three consecutive nights. On Wednesday, June 29, the first one was held at the Village Theatre in Westwood, the second at the Encino Theatre in Encino, and the last at the West Coast Theatre in Long Beach. These theaters were chosen because they had the dual optical equipment necessary to show the picture. Someone from the studio was on hand to supervise the projection.

Wanger thought that the three previews proved they had a powerful piece of entertainment on their hands. The Allied Artists executives felt otherwise, obviously, for it was after the previews that they insisted on removing the humor from the movie. As far as they were concerned, humor and horror didn't mix.

On his own, before the frame story was added, Wanger showed the new cut of the picture to a preview audience at the Bay Theatre. It was a disaster. The audience was restless and many of them walked out. Wanger thought that the quality and humanity of the picture had been harmed by what he called "B-cutting" and the cards, which were the least complimentary, seemed to support his feelings.

All of this stuff about the sneak previews is documented quite well in the Walter Wanger files. Yet Kevin McCarthy told me another story which he said he got second hand from Ted Haworth, the film's production designer. According to Haworth, he and Siegel and Wanger took the work print to a theater in Long Beach and recorded the reaction of the audience, which they played for Steve Broidy the following Monday. The three thought they really had something. The audience was wildly enthusiastic. They screamed and laughed and screamed again. Broidy was furious. "Nobody gave you permission to do this!" he yelled and ordered them out of his office.

Another battle fought and lost was over the title of the film. Wanger never liked *The Body Snatchers*. He was afraid people would confuse his picture with the 1945 RKO film, *The Body Snatcher*, or so he told the executives at Allied Artists. He probably objected to it for a myriad of reasons.

Alberto Vargas, famous for his pin-up art, was working for the studio at the time, designing costumes and poster art for *World Without End* (1956). He suggested the following titles: *Fear, Inc.*, *Fatal Sleep*, *Fear Not My Love*, *Sleep into Oblivion*, *Sleep Not My Love*, and *The Unknown*.

Ted Haworth thought *Trail of Terror* might be a good title. *Out of the Darkness* and *The Ghouls* were also suggested.

Then the studio came up with a title they were quite pleased with — *They Came from Another World*, probably inspired by Universal-International's

It Came From Outer Space (1953). Wanger liked it better than *The Body Snatchers* so he agreed to it. Don Siegel thought it stank. He voiced his objection in a memo to Wanger dated September 21. "I've yet to find anyone, including the sales organization, publicity, who likes [the title]. I suggest two titles, both of which fit the picture like a glove, or, if you prefer, a pod, and they are: SLEEP NO MORE, and BETTER OFF DEAD."

When the studio heads didn't like either of Siegel's titles Wanger came up with a couple of his own — *Evil in the Night* and *World in Danger.* Broidy and Mirisch didn't like his titles either but since no one seemed to like *They Came from Another World*, they decided to call the film *Invasion of the Body Snatchers*. Dana Wynter begged Wanger to make them change their minds. She was afraid her parents would think she was demented if she appeared a film with that title.

Kevin McCarthy was shooting a television pilot in South Africa when he got the call from a disgruntled Don Siegel about the frame story that Steve Broidy wanted to tack onto the picture. Siegel had the right to be angry about it but look at the situation from Broidy's point of view. The mogul had a movie that he couldn't pigeonhole. Worse still, even the producer seemed to be having second and third thoughts about it. And when Wanger asked for the film to be shelved for a few months so he could get the bugs out of it, Broidy had had enough. That's when he came up with the idea for the new opening and closing.

In the frame story, Miles Bennell is in a hospital. We don't know how he got there but we assume the police brought him in because he was in the middle of the highway, screaming at people. Two policemen stand guard over him. The doctor on duty calls a psychiatrist and they, along with the two guards, listen to Miles' bizarre story. The doctor concludes that he's crazy, but the psychiatrist isn't so sure and while they're trying to figure out what to do with Miles an intern and an ambulance driver pass by with a badly injured man. The intern rolls him into the operating room while the driver explains what happened. The injured man ran his truck through a red light and was broadsided by a bus. "We had to dig him out from under the most peculiar things I ever saw," the ambulance driver remarks. "What things?" the psychiatrist asks. "I don't know what they are. I never saw them before. They looked like great big seed pods." When he tells the two doctors the truck was coming from Santa Mira, the psychiatrist tells the police to block all of the highways and call every law enforcement agency in the state. Then he phones the F.B.I. Miles, exhausted both physically and mentally, leans against the wall, and says, "Thank God" and the screen goes black.

At first Siegel refused to direct it. Daniel Mainwaring persuaded him to do it. Another director could make things even worse. So on September 16, on stage three at Allied Artists, Siegel shot the frame story. The outside of the hospital was actually the front of the studio. Whit Bissell, once considered for the role of Danny Kaufman, played the psychiatrist. The two police officers who accompanied him were Hubert Kerns and Morgan Windiel. Richard Deacon played the doctor and Betty Jo Renfro was his nurse. The ambulance driver was played by Robert Osterloh. Fred Fisher was the intern and the unconscious truck driver was played by Roger Cornwall. The two policemen who stood guard over Miles were Dave Kelly and Beau Anderson. All of them had to work without screen credit. The credits had already been shot and Allied Artists wasn't about to pay to do them over.

I may be in the minority, but I like the frame story. Had the picture gone out the way Siegel wanted it to, I think it would have been shocking, ground-breaking and horrifying but ultimately unsatisfying. I understand why Siegel wanted to end the movie the way he did. He felt it would drive the message home. *Be careful or you'll become a pod!* But Allied Artists wasn't in business to sell subtext; they sold entertainment. And when you think about it, Siegel still had his way. It's not the hopeless ending that he wanted, but it's an ambiguous ending. The crisis is still unresolved. We don't even know if the psychiatrist got through to the F.B.I.

The last and final blow to the film came when Steve Broidy decided to release it in a wide screen process known as SuperScope. During the 1950s, 20th Century Fox had a patent on CinemaScope, a wide screen process which used an anamorphic lens to squash the image during filming and to stretch it again during projection. Fox charged $25,000 for the use of the lens. Superscope offered a much cheaper alternative. Movies were shot using regular lenses. The image was cropped and squashed during the printing and stretched out again when it was projected. Knowing in advance that the image would be cropped, cameramen were mindful to leave plenty of space at the top and bottom of the frame. Ellsworth Fredericks had composed *The Body Snatchers* for the standard 1 to 1.85 ratio. SuperScope had a 2 to 1 ratio, which meant that more of the image had to be cropped than was intended. The result was anything but pleasing.

On the plus side, when the 16mm prints of the film were released to television, they were made from the original full frame negative. Television viewers saw more of the image than anyone ever saw theatrically. Unfortunately, the prints released to television in the mid-70s panned and scanned the Superscope image, destroying the composition and boosting the grain. I would say it's impossible to watch if I wasn't living in an age when people are happy to watch images stretched out of the shape on their wide screen TVs.

Wanger didn't see the Superscope version of the film until December. He wasn't happy about it.

CHAPTER SEVEN

THE MOVIE

What you are about to read is a transcription (from memory I am ashamed to say) of the *Body Snatchers*. It is *not* the screenplay. It's more like a cutting continuity with annotations. It is the closest you'll get to being at one of those preview screenings over fifty years ago, before the humor was cut from the movie and the frame story was added. It's kind of like watching the movie with Don Siegel.

For your sake, I am going to assume that you don't know this film by heart: so, for easy identification, all of the dialogue and scenes that were cut from the movie appear in boldface. Background information and personal observations are in italics.

Certain abbreviations have been used: ext. *(exterior)*, int. *(interior)* f.g. *(foreground)*, b.g. *(background)* o.s. *(off stage)*, p.o.v. *(point of view)*.

Get some popcorn and a soda and get started.

EXT. SMALL EMERGENCY HOSPITAL — NIGHT

This is a small hospital on a quiet street. A lighted sign tells us this is an emergency hospital. Approaching fast, with siren blaring, is a police car. It stops in front of the hospital. DR. EMMETT HILL and two state policemen get out of the car and scurry into the hospital.

INT. HALLWAY — FULL SHOT

The doctor and the two policemen enter the hospital with a sense of urgency. A nurse sits in a small reception office behind a glass window, engaged in a conversation with DR. BASSETT. As soon as he sees Hill, Bassett cuts his conversation short and quickly makes his way out of the little room to greet the doctor.

DR. BASSETT: Dr. Hill

DR. HILL: Dr. Bassett. Well, where's the patient?

DR. BASSETT: I hated to drag you out of bed at this time of night.

The two doctors leave the two policemen behind and Hill follows Bassett down the hall to one of the rooms.

DR. HILL: That's all right.

From beyond the door comes the frantic voice of DR. MILES BENNELL.

MILES: *(yelling)* Will you let me go while there's still time?

DR. BASSETT: You'll soon see why I did.

Bassett throws the door open and we see Miles. His clothes are torn and dirty. He breaks free from the grip of two husky policemen and grabs Bassett. The policemen pull Miles back into the room.

MILES: *(wildly to Bassett)* Doctor! Will you tell these fools I'm not crazy? Make them listen to me before it's too late.

DR. HILL: I'll listen to you. *(steps into the room)* Let him go.

The policemen hesitate, then, at a nod from Dr. Bassett, they release him. Miles eyes Dr. Hill suspiciously.

MILES: Who are you?

DR. HILL: I'm Doctor Hill from the State Mental Hospital.

At his wit's end Miles covers his face and is again restrained by the two officers who think he's going to attack the doctor again.

MILES: *I am not insane!*

DR. HILL: *(angrily)* Let him go!

The two officers back off and Miles attempts to collect himself. In a softer but no less desperate voice he continues.

MILES: Doctor, now you must listen to me. You must understand me. I'm a doctor too. I am not insane. I am not insane. I...

DR. HILL: All right. All right. Now suppose we just sit down over here, Dr. Bennell, and you tell me what happened.

Dr. Hill steers Miles back into the room and the two of them sit on the couch. Now that he's found someone willing to listen, Miles settles in. After taking a deep breath he begins his story.

MILES: Well it started - — for me it started last Thursday.

RIPPLE TO FLASHBACK
EXT. SANTA MIRA TRAIN DEPOT — DAY

A Streamliner is picking up speed as it draws out of the rural station. Miles crosses the tracks toward the platform.

MILES: *(narration)* In response to an urgent message from my nurse I'd hurried home from a medical convention I'd been attending. At first glance everything looked the same. It wasn't. Something evil had taken possession of the town.

Note: This business about an urgent message is something that was cooked up for the narration to give a sense of urgency to the proceedings. It is not supported by anything that follows. Miles is surprised to hear that he has "an office full of patients."

Miles approaches the BAGGAGEMAN who has a cart full of suitcases.

MILES: These two. *(gives handler his claim check and a tip)* Here you are.

HANDLER: Thank you, sir. There you are.

MILES: *(grabs his baggage)* Thank you.

Miles carries his suitcases up the stairs to the platform and gives a friendly greeting to someone he knows as they pass each other.

ANGLE ON SALLY WITHERS

Miles' pretty nurse, walking up the ramp to the platform. She waves to Miles.

Note: Sally doesn't have a name in Finney's serial. She's simply referred to as his nurse. There is no description of her and she plays no part in the story whatsoever. In the first draft screenplay Mainwaring describes her as a hundred and fifteen pounds of yellow, wind-blown hair and prime flesh poured into sweater and skirt, a characterization better suited to one of his hard-boiled detective novels. In the first cut of the film, the camera panned with Sally as she rushed up the ramp to greet Miles. To speed up the pace, the scene picks up in the middle of the pan. The director approved of the cut, but was nevertheless sorry that the audience would no longer get to see her bouncing bosom.

SALLY: Doc!

MILES: Hiya, Sally.

She throws her arms around him.

SALLY: Hi. Welcome home. I'm glad you're back.

MILES: How's Mickey and the baby?

SALLY: Oh, they're fine but it seems that everyone else in Santa Mira needs a doctor. You've got an office full of patients.

MILES: Oh no! On my first day back?

She opens the door so that he can put his bags in the back seat of the car.

SALLY: Well, some of them have been waiting for two weeks.

MILES: Why didn't you send them to Pursey or Carmichael like I told you to do?

SALLY: Most of them wouldn't go. They wanted to see you.

Sally gets into the car; Miles slides behind the wheel.

MILES: Oh. What's the matter with them?

SALLY: They wouldn't say.

They drive off.

INT. CAR — PROCESS — MOVING

The dirt road winds through rolling farm country.

SALLY: You know usually people can't talk enough about what's ailing them.

MILES: Uh huh.

SALLY: For instance, Wally Eberhard was in twice and called three times about something but he wouldn't tell me what it was.

MILES: That's funny.

SALLY: Neither would anyone else from Becky Driscoll down to that fat traffic cop, Sam Janzek.

MILES: Becky Driscoll? I thought she was in England.

Note: This line was added to explain why a woman who was born and raised in California would have a British accent.

Though he attempted to make his remark casual, Sally is onto him and grins.

SALLY: She got back a few days ago and she wanted to see you. Are you still interested?

MILES: My interest in married women is strictly professional or yours would have been a lost cause long ago.

SALLY: *(laughs)* How was the convention?

MILES: Wonderful. They wept with envy when I read my paper.

EXT. ROAD — FRUIT STAND

It's vacant and shabby with empty boxes strewn about. Into the road dashes a nine-year old boy, JIMMY GRIMADLI, right into the path of Miles' car. Miles slams on the brakes just in time.

The boy, crying hysterically, keeps on running as though the devil was at his heels. Emerging from the lane, yelling at him, is his mother, ANNA GRIMALDI.

ANNA: Jimmy! Come back here! Jimmy!

Still shaken, Miles jumps out of the car and races up the road to Mrs. Grimaldi.

MILES: What's the matter, Mrs. Grimaldi?

ANNA: Oh nuthin', he just don't want to go to school.

MILES: Well, if I were you I'd have a talk with his teacher.

ANNA: I will when I get time.

Miles notices the vegetable stand.

MILES: What's the matter, Joe been sick?

ANNA: *(detached)* No, he gave the stand up. Too much work.

MILES: Oh.

Anna starts after her child again only with less urgency. Sally drives forward and Miles gets back into the car and drives on.

Note: In the first cut of the film, the camera returned to the int. of the car before Miles settled into his seat. But the image on the process screen wasn't steady so Siegel asked Richard Heermance to make the cut after the car was already in motion so that the image on the screen wouldn't look as phony.

MILES: *(narration)* The boy's panic should have told me it was more than school he was afraid of. And that littered, closed up vegetable stand should have told me something too. When I last saw it less than a month ago it was the cleanest and busiest stand on the road.

INT. CAR — MILES AND SALLY — PROCESS

SALLY: That's strange. She was in to see you too, last Friday, and I tried to get her to see Doc Pursey but she wouldn't. She said only you could help her.

MILES: Well, whatever it was it couldn't have been too serious I guess.

DISSOLVE TO
MILES' INNER OFFICE — AT THE WINDOW —
CLOSE ON X-RAY — DAY

For a few seconds Miles's face his hidden by the x-ray he's holding.

Note: In the first cut of the film Miles stood at the window and then raised the x-ray into the shot. Siegel felt it would be more effective to see the x-ray first.

MILES: One minor concussion, two cases of the common cold, and six cancelled appointments. Looks like you rushed me here for nothing.

SALLY: *(joining him at the window)* I don't understand it Miles. They couldn't wait to see you. But you're still booked up solid for the afternoon.

MILES: Mmmm, bet they don't show. *(raises the window shade)* Look.

MAIN STREET — THEIR P.O.V.

Amidst the activity on the sidewalk we see one man talking to another and a couple walking across the street.

MILES' VOICE: *(o.s.)* There's Wally Eberhard talking somebody into buying some insurance. There's nothing wrong with him. And Bill Bittner's taking his secretary to lunch.

INT. MILES' OFFICE — MED. SHOT

A bell RINGS o.s. Someone has entered the office. Sally starts for the double doors to the reception room.

MILES: And speaking of lunch would you tell whoever that is that I'm out having mine?

Miles is at the door to the hall with his hand on the knob when he hears a female voice.

BECKY: *(o.s.)* Is Dr. Bennell in?

SALLY: *(o.s.)* Uh — yes, he's here.

BECKY: *(o.s.)* Do you suppose he has time to see me?

SALLY: *(o.s.)* Well if he hasn't there's something wrong with him. Go right in.

Miles sighs, resigned to the fact that he may miss his lunch. He's on his way back to the reception room when BECKY DRISCOLL appears at the double doors in a strapless summer dress. The two old friends smile warmly at one another and shake hands.

MILES: Becky. Almost five years.

BECKY: It's wonderful to be home again. I've been away so long I feel almost like a stranger in my own country. I hope you don't mind my coming in without an appointment.

Sally is sitting at her desk, watching the two of them with interest. Miles closes the curtained double doors to give them some privacy. He offers Becky a chair with a gesture and leans against an examination table.

MILES: Not at all. What'll you have? We're pushing appendectomies this week.

BECKY: *(laughs)* Oh, Miles!

MILES: I don't know. Maybe I clown around too much. Pretty soon my patients won't trust me to prescribe aspirin for them. Now seriously, what's the trouble?

Becky pauses for a moment, looking at her lap, not quite sure how to begin.

BECKY: It's my cousin.

MILES: Wilma? What's the matter with her?

BECKY: She has a — well I guess you'd call it a delusion. You know her uncle, Uncle Ira?

MILES: Sure. I'm his doctor.

BECKY: Well, Miles, she's got herself thinking he isn't her uncle.

MILES: How do you mean, that they're not really related?

BECKY: No. She thinks he's an imposter or something, someone who only looks like Ira.

MILES: Have you seen him?

BECKY: I just came from there.

MILES: Well, is he Uncle Ira or isn't he Uncle Ira?

BECKY: Of course he is. I told Wilma that but it was no use. Please, could you stop by and have a talk with her?

MILES: Sally says I'm booked up for the afternoon but why don't you ask her to come in and see me?

BECKY: I'll try.

She rises and Miles escorts her to the door.

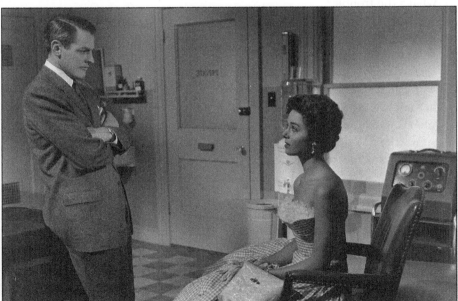

Above: Sally (Jean Willes) and Miles (Kevin McCarthy) are puzzled by all of the cancelled appointments. Below: "Well, is he Uncle Ira or isn't he Uncle Ira?" Miles asks Becky.

MILES: How about some lunch?
BECKY: I can't. I'm meeting Dad at the store.
He opens the door for her and follows her into the hall.

INT. HALL — TRUCKING SHOT — MILES AND BECKY

They negotiate their way down the hallway to the stairs.
MILES: When did you get back?
BECKY: I came back from London two months ago. I've been in Reno.
MILES: Reno?
BECKY: Reno. Dad tells me you were there too.
MILES: Five months ago.
BECKY: Oh! I'm sorry.
Miles helps her with her sweater as they walk down the stairs.
MILES: So was I. I wanted it to work. Well, I guess that makes us lodge brothers now.
BECKY: Yes.
MILES: Except that I'm paying dues while you collect them.
BECKY: *(laughs)* Miles!

Note: Everything starting with "Oh! I'm sorry" was added on the set.

EXT. MILES' OFFICE BUILDING — DAY

In f.g. the fat traffic cop that Sally mentioned earlier, SAM JANZEK, stands beside a car writing out a ticket. His three-wheeled motorcycle is alongside the car. In b.g. Miles and Becky come out of the building and Miles greets a gentleman passing by on the sidewalk. As they come to the curb, Janzek puts the ticket under the windshield wiper and, mounting the bike, kicks the motor on.
MILES: Sam.
SAM: Hello, Doc.
MILES: At it again, eh? My nurse tells me you were in last week and wanted very much to see me.
SAM: It wasn't anything important.
Janzek rides off. Miles looks after him, puzzled.
BECKY: Say, didn't he go to college with us?
Hooking her arm, Mile steers her across the street.
MILES: Quit his second year to get married, like I wanted us to do.
BECKY: Just be thankful I didn't take you seriously.

MILES: You be thankful. I found out that a doctor's wife needs the understanding of an Einstein and the patience of a saint.

BECKY: And love?

They reach the other side of the street and pause in front of the hardware store owned by Becky's father.

MILES: I wouldn't know about that. I'm just a general practitioner. Love is handled by the specialists.

BECKY: Well, here's where I leave you.

She offers him her hand. He gives it an affectionate squeeze and holds on when she starts off.

MILES: You know something? This is where you left me the last time.

She throws him a smile and goes into the store. Miles goes off to find some lunch. A child passes by and he pats the boy's head.

MILES: Hi, Johnny.

DISSOLVE TO

EXT. — STREET CLOCK OUTSIDE OF MILES' OFFICE
It's 4:45.
Note: This is a freeze frame.

INT. MILES' OFFICE — LATE AFTERNOON —
CLOSE SHOT — MILES

He steps away from the closet, putting on his coat as he goes to the double doors. Sally is at her desk in the reception room.

MILES: Sally, I'm off. Will you tell the answering service I'll be at home?

SALLY: Good night, Doc.

MILES: Good night.

He starts for the door when he's stopped in his tracks by Jimmy Grimaldi's tearful voice.

JIMMY: *(o.s.)* I'm not going in there.

Jimmy, in tears, is dragged into the reception room by his GRANDMOTHER. He struggles to get away.

GRANDMOTHER: Stop all of this nonsense and be a good boy. Come on.

Jimmy breaks from her grasp but Miles catches him before he can escape.

MILES: Hey! Hey! Hey! Take it easy. *(places his hands on the boy's shoulders)* Isn't this Jimmy Grimaldi?

GRANDMOTHER: Yes, doctor. Can I talk to you a moment?

MILES: Sure. *(to Jimmy)* You know I almost ran you down this morning. You've got to be more careful when you run out in the road.

JIMMY: Almost ran me down.

MILES: Come on.

GRANDMOTHER: Come on.

Miles leads the way to his office. Again the boy breaks free and runs smack into Sally's waiting arms. She holds him tight.

MILES: Hey! Hey! Hey! Hey! Hey! Hey! Slow down now. *(crouches low so that he's eye level with Jimmy)* Look, school isn't as bad as all that. It can't be.

GRANDMOTHER: School isn't what upsets him. It's my daughter-in-law. He's got the crazy idea she isn't his mother.

Coming on the heels of his conversation with Becky about her cousin with a similar delusion, Miles is taken aback.

JIMMY: She isn't! She isn't! Don't let her get me!

SALLY: Nobody's going to get you, Jimmy.

Miles gets on his feet and with a nod of his head signals the grandmother to follow him into his office, CAMERA moving with them. Miles takes a bottle from a shelf and shakes a capsule into his hand.

MILES: *(softly)* How long has this been going on?

GRANDMOTHER: An hour ago I found him hiding in the cellar, having hysterics. He wouldn't tell me anything until I started to phone his mother. That's when he said Anna wasn't his mother.

MILES: Could you keep him with you for a day or so?

GRANDMOTHER: Of course.

MILES: *(gives her the bottle)* Give him one of these, every four hours during the day, and call me tomorrow and let me know how he's feeling.

GRANDMOTHER: Yes, Doctor. Thank you.

Miles fills a paper cup with water from the cooler.

JIMMY: *(o.s.)* Don't let her get me!

SALLY: *(o.s.)* Nobody's going to get you, Jimmy.

Note: These two lines were lifted from the soundtrack of the earlier scene and repeated.

The grandmother follows Miles as he returns to the reception room. He stoops down to give Jimmy the pill.

MILES: *(cheerfully)* All right, Jimmy, open your mouth and shut your eyes, and in the words of the poet I'll give you something to make you wise.

Once Jimmy has the pill in his mouth, Miles tilts the cup and gives him some water to wash it down.

SALLY: That's a good boy, Jimmy.

JIMMY: *(firmly)* I'm not going home, ever.

Miles confirms Jimmy's resolve with a little shake of his fist and rises.

MILES: You're going to stay at your grandmother's house. *(to Sally)* Would you call his mother and tell her…

JIMMY: *(screaming)* She's not my mother! Don't tell her where I am!

MILES: All right. All right. All right. Run along. Everything's going to be all right. *(gives Jimmy a pat on the butt)* You be a good boy now.

GRANDMOTHER: *(on her way out the door)* Good night, Doctor.

Once they've gone Miles turns to Sally.

MILES: Sally, I've changed my mind. I'm not going directly home. I'm going to stop off and see Wilma Lentz.

SALLY: Shall I call the boy's mother?

MILES: Yes, call her and tell her what happened and that I suggested it might be a good idea if the boy spend the night at his grandmother's house.

Miles goes back to his office, leaving Sally to search through her index cards for Anna Grimaldi's phone number.

DISSOLVE TO

EXT. — THE LENTZ HOME — LATE AFTERNOON

It is a tree-lined street, with old houses standing well back from the sidewalk. Miles' car pulls into Ira Lentz's driveway. Becky and WILMA LENTZ are sitting on the swing on the lawn. The garage door is open. It's a mess inside. The workbench is untidy and the car is filthy. IRA LENTZ is standing at the work bench. He steps out to greet Miles.

IRA: *(cheerfully)* You're back, Doc, so watch the death rate go up. Kill many today?

MILES: *(shaking hands)* Bagged the limit. Your sacroiliac been bothering you again?

IRA: No. Not since you put it back in place.

MILES: Then get busy with that lawn mower.

IRA: More you cut it, the faster it grows. But I suppose it's got to be done some time.

He goes back into the garage. Miles heads for the porch.

Note: Siegel wrestled with this sequence for quite a while. He didn't like the way it played for one reason or another. At one point he cut everything but Ira's last line, but in the end the whole thing hit the cutting room floor.

ANGLE ON MILES

He walks across the lawn to the swing where Becky and Wilma are waiting for him. Wilma is a solid, pink-cheeked, un-complicated woman in her early forties.

WILMA: Hello, Miles.

MILES: Nice to see you Wilma. Becky.

WILMA: Let's have it. You talked to him. What do you think?

MILES: It's him. He's your Uncle Ira all right.

WILMA: He is not.

END OF REEL ONE

Miles turns to look at Ira who is mowing the lawn some distance away.

MILES: How's he different?

WILMA: **I've been waiting till he'd get a haircut. There's a little scar on the back of Uncle Ira's neck. He had a boil there.**

MILES: **I know. I lanced it.**

WILMA: **You can't see the scar when he needs a haircut. Today he got one.**

MILES: **And the scar's gone?**

WILMA: **No. It's there.**

MILES: **Then how is he different?**

WILMA: That's just it; there is no difference you can actually see. He looks, sounds, acts, and remembers like Uncle Ira.

MILES: Then he is your Uncle Ira. Can't you see that? No matter how you feel he is.

WILMA: But he isn't. There's something missing. He's been a father to me since I was a baby. Always when he talked to me there was a special look in his eye. That look's gone.

MILES: What about memories? There must be certain things that only you and he would know about.

WILMA: *(frustrated)* Oh there are. I've talked to him about them. He remembers them all down to the last small detail, just like Uncle Ira would. But Miles, there's no emotion. None. Just the pretense of it. The words, the gestures, the tone of voice — everything else is the same, but not the feeling. *(firmly)* Memories or not he isn't my Uncle Ira.

MILES: Wilma, I'm on your side. Now my business is people in trouble and I'm going to find a way to help you. Now no one could possibly impersonate your Uncle Ira without you or your Aunt Aleda or even me seeing a million little differences. I want you to realize that, think about it, and you'll know that the trouble is inside you.

Above: "An hour ago I found him hiding in the cellar, having hysterics. He wouldn't tell me anything until I started to phone his mother. That's when he said that Anna wasn't his mother," Grandma Grimaldi (Beatrice Maude) tells Miles. Below: "Let's have it. You talked to him. What do you think?" Wilma asks Miles.

AUNT ALEDA: *(o.s.)* Wilma, where are you?

WILMA: Out on the lawn. *(to Miles)* Say nothing to her.
Miles reassuringly pats her knee.

Note: This sequence was photographed in a standard way, alternating between a master three shot and close-ups of Miles, Wilma, and Becky. When Miles assures Wilma that her Uncle Ira is the real McCoy, and she emphatically states that he isn't, the editor chose to play the moment in the master three shot. Siegel wanted Wilma's response in a close-up to give the line more punch. The editor wasn't sure he'd be able to smoothly work his way back into the master. The solution was simple. With one exception, the entire sequence is played in close-ups. Becky's reaction close-ups were eliminated altogether. Until they cut back to the master you forget she's even there.

ANGLE ON AUNT ALEDA crossing the lawn to join them. She is a small, dumpy, grey woman.

AUNT ALEDA: *(pleasantly)* Why Miles, I didn't know you were here.
Welcome home.

MILES: Hello Mrs. Lentz.

AUNT ALEDA: *(to Wilma)* Did you ask Miles to stay for dinner?

MILES: I can't tonight.

AUNT ALEDA: I'm making spoon bread.

Note: Aunt Aleda's Spoon Bread recipe — 4 eggs, 1 quart milk, 2 tablespoons butter (no substitutes), 1 teaspoon sugar, 1½ teaspoons salt, 1 cup corn meal. Heat oven to 425 F. Heat milk, stir in corn meal, sugar, and salt, stir until smooth and thick. Cover; cook until mushy. Remove from heat and add butter. Beat eggs till well blended and slowly stir into mush. Pour into well-greased 1½-quart casserole. Bake, uncovered, 50 to 55 minutes. Makes 4 to 5 servings.

MILES: Please, don't tempt me.

AUNT ALEDA: Well, maybe next time. Wilma, where are my glasses?

BECKY: I think I saw them on the mantelpiece. *(rises)* I'll go with you.
Becky walks off with Aunt Aleda. Miles takes a seat on the swing next to Wilma.

MILES: **Your Aunt Aleda would know! She couldn't be fooled, of all people. Have you talked with her, told her about this?**
Wilma shakes her head no.

MILES: **Why not?**
WILMA: **Because she's not my Aunt.**

FAR SHOT — UNCLE IRA mowing the lawn.
TWO SHOT — MILES AND WILMA

For a moment they share an awkward silence.
WILMA: Miles, am I going crazy. Don't spare me. I've got to know.
MILES: No you're not. Even these days it isn't as easy to go crazy as you might think. But you don't have to be losing your mind to need psychiatric help. I'd like you to see a doctor friend of mine.
WILMA: Psychiatrist?
MILES: Dan Kaufman. I'll make an appointment for you tomorrow.
WILMA: *(sighs)* All right. But it's a waste of time. There's nothing wrong with me. *(looks off at Ira)* We'd better break this up or he'll start wondering.
She slides off the swing and Miles follows her lead. Becky returns.
MILES: *(confused)* Wondering what?
WILMA: If I don't suspect. You've been a big help and I don't want you to worry about me. *(to Becky)* Or you either. I'll be all right.
MILES: Sure you will. Staying here Becky or may I drive you home?
BECKY: Would you like me to stay?
WILMA: Of course not. Good night.
MILES: Good night.
Miles and Becky walk across the lawn together, passing Ira on the way.
IRA: *(with a wink)* Nice having Becky back again, eh boy?
MILES: *(gives him a friendly pat on the shoulder)* Sure is.

Note: Miles' last line is what is known as a wild line, a piece of dialog added later, usually for clarification. Apparently, Siegel felt Miles' pat on the shoulder wasn't enough of a response.

MILES: *(narration)* In the back of my mind a warning bell was ringing. Sick people who couldn't wait to see me then suddenly were perfectly all right. A boy who said his mother wasn't his mother. A woman who said her uncle wasn't her uncle. But I didn't listen. Obviously the boy's mother was his mother, I'd seen her. And Uncle Ira was Uncle Ira. There was no doubt of that that after I talked to him.

Note: Because of the cut, the audience is left to wonder when it was that Miles had this talk with Ira. I guess we're supposed to assume he had such a talk. It might have been a good idea to have Miles moving away from Ira during the dissolve at the beginning of the scene. As it stands he's halfway across the lawn when the scene opens.

During the narration the camera cuts to Wilma sadly watching them go and Ira stuffing his pipe into his mouth, smiling as he watches Becky and Miles drive off.

Note: This is one of the creepiest moments in the movie. Somebody once asked Siegel how he managed to accomplish this when on the surface there doesn't seem to be anything sinister going on. He said he didn't know.

INT. MILES' CAR — MILES AND BECKY — PROCESS

Becky looks worried.

BECKY: Miles, he is Ira?

MILES: Of course he is. What do you mean?

BECKY: It's just that Wilma's so positive. Will she be all right?

MILES: Oh I think so. I'm a doctor according to my diploma but I don't really know what Wilma's trouble is. I could start talking psychiatrical jargon but it's out of my line and in Dan Kaufman's. I wish you didn't have to go home for dinner.

BECKY: I don't. Dad's eating out with a friend.

MILES: I could pick you up at seven.

BECKY: Well...

MILES: It's summer and the moon is full, and "I know a bank where the wild thyme grows."

BECKY: *(she's heard this one before and happily joins him at the tail end)* "...where the wild thyme grows." *(laughs)* You haven't changed a bit.

DISSOLVE TO

EXT. SKY TERRACE INN PARKING LOT —

MILES AND BECKY — NIGHT

They walk slowly past a few cars in the parking lot, toward the stairs to the restaurant, when a convertible almost backs into them. Miles jumps back, pulling Becky with him.

MILES: Whup! Woah! Watch out!

There are two men in the convertible. DR. DANIEL KAUFMAN, a well-built man in his thirties, is at the wheel. Sitting beside him is DR. ED PURSEY, an elderly, serious, slow-speaking country doctor and Miles' only competition in Santa Mira.

DANNY: Sorry. Hey, Miles! When did you get back?

MILES: This morning. How are you Danny? This is Miss Driscoll. Dr. Kaufman, our one and only psychiatrist. *(cautions Becky)* Watch out what you say. Ed, you remember Becky.

DR. PURSEY: I should. I brought her into the world.

DANNY: You did us all a favor.

BECKY: Hello, Dr. Pursey.

MILES: This saves me a phone call. I've got a mixed-up kid and a woman who need a witch doctor.

DANNY: *(almost bored)* The boy says his father isn't his father and the woman says her sister isn't her sister.

Miles isn't sure what to make of Danny's near accurate remark.

MILES: That's pretty close. I knew you'd been studying hypnosis but when did you start reading minds?

DR. PURSEY: He doesn't have to read them. I've sent him a dozen patients since it started.

MILES: Well, what is it? What's going on?

DANNY: I don't know, a strange neurosis, evidently contagious, an epidemic mass hysteria. In two weeks it's spread all over town.

MILES: What causes it?

DANNY: Worry about what's going on in the world probably. **Instead of seeing flying saucers, everybody and his brother are deluding themselves that their cousins and their uncles and their aunts aren't.**

Note: As often happens when lines are cut, it throws the continuity off. Dr. Pursey's head radically shifts position between the two angles where this cut was made.

MILES: Make room for Wilma Lentz tomorrow, will you Danny?

DANNY: Send her in around two. *(to Becky)* **Are you quite sure this gentleman you're with is what he seems he seems?**

BECKY: **Suddenly I'm not sure of anything.**

DANNY: Good night.

MILES: So long, Danny.

Danny and Pursey drive off. Miles and Becky walk up the stairs to the nightclub.

MILES: This is the oddest thing I ever heard of. Let's hope we don't catch it. I'd hate to wake up some morning and find out that you weren't you.

BECKY: *(laughs)* I'm not the high school kid you used to romance so how can you tell?

MILES: You really want to know?

BECKY: Uh huh.

With that he pulls her into his arms and kisses her.

MILES: Mmmmm. You're Becky Driscoll.

Note: This is precisely the way that he discovers that she's no longer Becky at the end of the movie.

She smiles and brushes his nose with her own. As they walk up the steps they hear music coming from the nightclub.

BECKY: Hey, Santa Mira's looking up.

MILES: Has ever since you got back.

BECKY: Is this an example of your bedside manner, Doctor?

MILES: No ma'am. That comes later.

Note: These last four lines were ad-libbed. According to Kevin McCarthy, Don Siegel encouraged the actors to add a little humor whenever they could, as long as it wasn't incongruous.

They enter the nightclub.

INT. SKY TERRACE INN — DINING ROOM — NIGHT

The PROPRIETOR, delighted by the appearance of some customers, steps briskly across the sparsely occupied Dining Room to greet Becky and Miles who have just stepped in to the Cocktail Lounge.

PROPRIETOR: Good evening, Doctor.

MILES: *(a little surprised)* What happened to the crowd tonight?

PROPRIETOR: I don't know. It's been this way for two or three weeks now.

MILES: *(removing Becky's wrap)* Well, at least we don't have to wait for a table.

OWNER: Take your pick, here *(motions)* or here?

MILES: Here I think. *(gives the Proprietor Becky's wrap)* Shall we?

BECKY: Uh huh.

Beyond the small dance floor is a bandstand, but no musicians. The music is coming from the jukebox.

MILES: Where's the band?

OWNER: Business started falling off so I had to let them go. There's the jukebox though.

MILES: Shall we dance? *(they dance cheek to cheek)* I hope you didn't let the bartender go.

OWNER: I'm the bartender. Martinis?

MILES: Two, dry. Uh, very dry.

BECKY: Miles?

MILES: Um.

BECKY: I don't care what Dr. Kaufman says, I'm worried.

A phone rings in b.g. The Proprietor, who is behind the bar, mixing drinks, answers it.

MILES: You are in the capable hands of your personal physician.

PROPRIETOR: Oh, Doctor.

Miles sighs with a resignation of a man who has had his evenings spoiled more than once.

MILES: There's our evening. Sorry.

He and Becky go to the bar and Miles takes the phone from the Proprietor.

MILES: Dr. Bennell.

OPERATOR: *(filtered)* Jack Belicec wants you to come to his house right away, Doctor. He says it's urgent.

MILES: Thank you. *(hangs up phone)* Better hold those drinks. Emergency. Well, at least they called before we ordered dinner. How hungry are you?

BECKY: I can wait.

MILES: It may be quite a while.

BECKY: Then I'll go with you.

MILES: *(to Proprietor)* Sorry. We'll be back later.

They walk off leaving the Proprietor with two martinis and no one to drink them.

DISSOLVE TO

EXT. LANE LEADING TO JACK BELICEC'S HOUSE — NIGHT

As Miles' car approaches the driveway, the headlights sweep across the plaque on the brick fence that reads BELICEC.

INT. CAR — SHOOTING FROM BACK SEAT — PROCESS

Through the windshield we see a one-story frame house with a garage attached. The approaching lights of Miles' car center on a tall, intense man of forty standing in front of the garage. He is JACK BELICEC.

MILES: There's Jack.

Note: Another wild line.

END OF REEL TWO

EXT. — ANGLE ON CAR — NIGHT

Miles gets out of the car with his medical bag, leaving Becky behind. CAMERA follows him as he approaches Jack.

MILES: Hello, Jack. What's the matter, Teddy sick?

JACK: No.

THEODORA BELICEC runs out of the house in a frantic state. She takes hold of Jack.

TEDDY: Miles, thank heaven! I thought you'd never get here!

(o.s.) We hear the slam of the car door and a few seconds later Becky joins them.

MILES: Well, if you're not sick who is?

JACK: Nobody.

MILES: *(nettled)* Then why did you drag me away from my dinner?

JACK: You won't believe it, Miles, until you see it for yourself. Hello, Becky. Good to see you again.

TEDDY: Hi, Becky.

BECKY: Hi, Teddy.

Teddy puts her arm around Becky. They enter the garage and stand in front of the door to the PLAYROOM.

JACK: Would you be willing to forget that you're a doctor for a while?

MILES: Why?

JACK: I don't want you to call the police right away.

MILES: Quit acting like a writer. What's going on?

JACK: Maybe you can tell me. You're the doctor.

INT. PLAYROOM — FROM BILLIARD TABLE

The light over the table is off and it is in comparative darkness. In b.g. to the left is a bar, there is a small lamp on a table next to the door and the light is on. There are several chairs here and there. On the right, in front of the wall that divides the room, is Jack's desk and typewriter. Above the desk there's a cuckoo clock. On the wall behind the pool table are enlarged, framed book covers from Jack's mystery novels. The four enter, and Jack closes the door. Teddy and Becky stop at the bar. Jack stands beside them.

JACK: Miles — uh — put the light on over the pool table.

Miles sets his medical bag on one of the barstools and goes to the table. He pulls the light cord. Stretched out on the table, covered by a rubberized sheet, is a body. Miles pauses for a moment and turns to Jack.

JACK: Go on, pull it down.

Miles pulls back the sheet to reveal a man's head and naked upper torso. He glances back at Jack then lifts the head, studies it a moment, then turns his attention to one of the arms. During his examination Jack slowly approaches him, lighting his pipe, leaving Teddy and Becky at the bar. Becky moves closer but still keeps her distance, stopping near the cuckoo clock.

MILES: Who is he?

JACK: I have no idea. **It was in the closet where I keep my old manuscripts. A while ago I came to look through them, and there it was, lying on top of the cartons, stark naked. I put it here. Want to call the cops?**

MILES: **No. Not yet.**

JACK: **Why not?**

Miles doesn't answer.

JACK: **It isn't just an ordinary body, is it?**

MILES: **I never saw one like it. It looks unused.**

Note: Jack's last line and Miles' response survive in the trailer.

CUT TO ANGLE ON CUCKOO CLOCK sounding off, startling Becky. She moves closer to the table.

BECKY: It's face, Miles, it's vague.

JACK: It's like first impression that's stamped on a coin. It isn't finished.

MILES: You're right. It has all the features but no detail, no character, no lines.

JACK: It's no dead man

MILES: Have you got an inkpad around the house?

JACK: Should be one in the desk, why?

MILES: I want to take the corpse's fingerprints.

Jack goes to the desk, finds and ink pad and a piece of paper and gives them to Miles.

BECKY: Of course it's a dead man. What else could it be?

MILES: *(glances thoughtfully at the body)* I don't know but I've got a feeling that…well, it sounds crazy, but if I should do an autopsy, *(begins inking the fingers)* I think I'd find every organ in perfect condition, just as perfect as the body is externally, everything in working order, all set to go. Hold that for me.

Jack puts the ink pad under the paper and holds it for Miles. Miles carefully takes the prints.

INSERT: INK-STAINED PAPER

There are no fingerprints on the paper — just smudges.
MILES: *(o.s.)* He's blank.

Note: Don Siegel complained that the fingerprints looked "fakey" and should be shot again. What do you suppose blank fingerprints should look like?

BACK TO SCENE

JACK: Waiting for the final finished face to be stamped onto it.
TEDDY: *(frightened)* But whose face? Tell me that.
MILES: I think we could all use a drink.

With his arm around Becky, Miles follows Jack to the bar. Jack gives Teddy a little kiss and steps behind the bar. Becky takes a seat. Miles remains standing.

JACK: Bourbon all right?
MILES: Fine.
TEDDY: Miles, answer me. Whose face?

Jack gathers three glasses and sets them in a straight line.

MILES: *(puts a friendly arm around Teddy's waist)* I haven't the slightest idea, honey, have you?
TEDDY: How tall would you say that thing is?
MILES: Oh, five ten, thereabouts.
TEDDY: How much does it weigh?
MILES: Mmmm, it's pretty thin, maybe a hundred and forty pounds.
TEDDY: Jack's five ten and weighs a hundred and forty pounds.

At this, Jack, startled by something that hadn't occurred to him, lets the bottle slip from his hand. It falls and he catches it as it breaks, cutting the palm of his hand.

JACK: Teddy, will you stop talking nonsense.
TEDDY: I'm sorry, darling.

Miles grabs his medical bag.

MILES: Come on, let's have that hand.

Jack steps to the end of the bar so that Miles and can treat his hand.

TEDDY: *(choked)* But it isn't nonsense! Becky, you don't think it's nonsense, do you?

BECKY: Well, of course it is. Jack's standing here in front of you.

JACK: Of course I am, bleeding to death. *(reaches around Becky to get his drink)* Excuse me.

INSERT: CUT HAND

Miles dabs the cut with a swab.

MILES: *(o.s.)* You know what? I'm afraid you may live.

RETURN TO SCENE

Miles applies a band aid to the cut.

BECKY: Miles don't you think we should call the police and have them take that dead body out of here?

MILES: I'm afraid it isn't just a dead body.

JACK: Thanks.

Jack wanders back to the pool table. Miles follows.

JACK: *(to body)* **Come to think of it, old Buddy, we do have a lot in common.**

MILES: *(thinking aloud)* I wonder if...

JACK: What?

MILES: I wonder if there's any connection.

JACK: What do you mean?

MILES: There's something strange going on in Santa Mira. Dr. Kaufman calls it an epidemic of mass hysteria. Becky's cousin's got it for one. She thinks that her uncle and her aunt aren't her uncle and her aunt.

Note: Because of the cut made in Wilma's sequence, this is the first time the audience hears that Wilma thinks her aunt is an imposter as well. There're several cases of such delusion. Well, this isn't you yet but there is a structural likeness. It's fantastic, but there must be some reason why this thing is in your house.

JACK: **Whatever it is, I don't like it.**

MILES: Would you be willing to sit up with your strange friend and see what his next move is?

JACK: **I was just going to suggest it.**

MILES: If nothing happens by morning call the police. If something happens, call me, will you?

JACK: You know I will.

Miles finishes his drink, sets it on the bar, and gives Teddy a hug.

MILES: Good night. Take it easy.

TEDDY: Sure.

Becky gives Teddy's hand a reassuring squeeze.

BECKY: Nothing's going to happen.

JACK: Well, if it does it'll make a charming, blood-curdling mystery story. **I hope I'm around to write it.**

As Miles and Becky exit

DISSOLVE TO

EXT. BECKY'S HOUSE — FULL SHOT — NIGHT

The windows of the two-story frame house are dark. Miles' car draws up at the curb. He and Becky get out of the car and cross the lawn to the front door.

MILES: *(narration)* I was careful not to let Becky know it, but for the first time I was really scared. Dan Kaufman's explanation for what was wrong in town, mass hysteria, couldn't explain away that body on Jack's pool table.

Note: Siegel wanted the narration to end just as Miles and Becky reach the porch. It doesn't.

Becky takes a key out of her bag and opens the front door.

INT. HALLWAY — TWO SHOT — MILES AND BECKY

Becky and Miles enter the dark house.

BECKY: Come in while I turn the lights on.

MILES: You're a forward wench, dragging me into a dark hallway to be kissed.

Becky flicks on the light. To the right there's a door that gives access to the basement.

BECKY: I'm dragging you into a dark hallway because I'm scared of the dark tonight.

MILES: In that case I'd better stay and tuck you in.

BECKY: That way lies madness.

Miles turns off the light.

MILES: What's wrong with madness?

Becky turns the light back on.

BECKY: Madness. Now goodnight.

They hear a noise from the basement and see a shadow on the wall as Becky's FATHER comes up the stairs, rolling down his shirtsleeves. He's a husky man with a kind face.

BECKY'S FATHER: *(cheerfully)* Well, it's about time you two got home.

BECKY: Dad, what are you doing in the basement this time of night?

BECKY'S FATHER: Working in my shop. How about a nightcap, Doc?

MILES: No thanks. It's kind of late. I'll take a rain check.

BECKY: Good night.

Becky goes up the stairs.

MILES: *(o.s.)* Good night.

BECKY'S FATHER: Night, Miles.

Becky's father turns off the light and follows Becky up the stairs.

DISSOLVE TO

INT. BELICEC'S PLAYROOM — NIGHT —

FULL SHOT FROM POOL TABLE

The light over the table is on. The body is still covered by the sheet, save for the head and its right hand. The face is no longer blank. It looks even more like Jack than it did before. In b.g. Jack sits with his elbow on the bar, his face resting against his hand, asleep. Teddy has her head on the bar. As we DISSOLVE IN, the cuckoo clock comes to life and wakes Teddy. As she slides off the stool and stretches, the eyes of the body open and stare blankly at the light over the table. Teddy approaches it with trepidation. When she sees that the eyes are open she is about to react until she notices something even more horrifying.

INSERT: CLOSE ON HAND

The palm of the hand has a wound identical to the one on Jack's hand and it's bleeding.

TEDDY screams and wakes Jack with a start. By the time he's on his feet Teddy is at his side, tugging on his arm.

TEDDY: *(hysterical)* Jack! It's you! It's you!

Jack takes a step toward the body but Teddy pulls him back.

TEDDY: No! No! You mustn't go near it! Get out of here, please! Please!

Her terror convinces Jack that this is the thing to do and they beat a hasty retreat.

Note: After Theodora screams at seeing the hand and tries to pull Jack out with her, the editor, Dick Heermance, CUT to a CLOSER SHOT of Jack and Theodora as they leave, eliminating as much footage of the fake head as he could. Siegel thought it was a good choice, making it less likely that audience would be aware that King Donovan was the body on the table at the beginning of the scene while another actor took his place in the b.g. with his back to the camera. Once Donovan wakes up the rubber replica replaces him on the table.

DISSOLVE TO
INT. MILES' LIVING ROOM — NIGHT

Jack pounds on the front door. Miles, in his robe and pajamas, rushes to the door and opens it. Jack, his arm around Theodora, enters with her. She is almost in a state of shock. He steers her to the couch and all but pushes her into the cushion.

Note: This is a low level angle. There is a table and lamp in the foreground on the left side of the screen. To balance the shot, the lamp is on the floor. It's something you're not supposed to notice.

MILES: What happened, Jack?
JACK: Teddy says that thing in our place is me right down to the cut on my hand. Sit down, baby. I didn't wait to look.
TEDDY: *(half out of her mind)* It's alive! It's alive! The hand was cut and bleeding and the position of the body had changed.
Conveniently, there's a bottle of booze on the coffee table. Miles fills a glass and hands it to her.
MILES: Here, take this. I'll call Danny Kaufman.
Miles hurries to the phone in the hall.

INT. HALLWAY

Miles sits down and dials Danny's number. He lights a cigarette while he waits for Danny to pick up.
DANNY'S VOICE: *(filtered)* Hello.
MILES: Hello, Danny?
DANNY'S VOICE: *(filtered)* Yeah.
MILES: Listen *(exaggeratedly solicitous)* did I wake you up?
DANNY'S VOICE: *(filtered) (curses like a wild man)*

MILES: Why, Doctor, where in the world did you learn such language? From your patients' foul and slimy subconscious, I suppose.

DANNY'S VOICE: *(filtered)* Miles, what do you want? I'm warning you, I'll hang up and leave the phone off the...

MILES: *(holding phone away from ear as tirade continues)* Okay, Danny. *(Note: This deleted exchange was something that was lifted almost word for word from Finney.)* Something's happened and I've gotta see you right away. Will you get over here as fast as you can? It's important.

DANNY'S VOICE: *(filtered)* Oh, okay.

Miles goes to the archway, separating the hall from the living room.

MILES: *(to the Belicecs)* He's on his way. I'll make some coffee and be right with you.

JACK: *(o.s.)* Good deal, Miles. Thanks.

Miles heads for the kitchen.

Note: When the 16mm prints were struck for television, Miles line "I'll make some coffee and be right with you" and Jack's reply was missing from the soundtrack. You could see Miles' mouth moving but nothing was coming out. It probably had something to do with it being at the end of the reel.

END OF REEL THREE

ANGLE ON KITCHEN WALL

We see Miles' shadow on the wall before he steps into scene to turn on the light.

JACK: *(o.s.)* Miles, what about Becky? Do you think she's all right?

Miles stops cold. He turns around and looks down the stairs leading to the basement. Becky's voice comes OVER the shot.

BECKY'S VOICE: *(o.s.)* Dad, what are you doing in the basement at this time of night?

BECKY'S FATHER'S VOICE: *(o.s.)* Working in my shop.

With that, Miles runs out of the kitchen into the back yard.

EXT. BACK PATIO — MED. SHOT AT BACK DOOR — NIGHT

Miles shoots out the door, gets into his car which is parked in the driveway, slams the door and, as he starts the motor and backs out we HEAR:

MILES: *(narration)* I don't know what it was, call it a premonition, but suddenly I had the feeling that Becky was in danger. I had to get to her as quickly as possible.

Note: In Finney's serial and novel, when Miles takes Becky home, she tells him that she doesn't think her father is her father. This is what makes Miles suddenly fear for her safety after Jack and Teddy show up at his place. In the film, Becky doesn't say anything about her father until much later, so something else had to trigger Miles' sudden concern. In the script, it's the open door to Miles' basement that makes him think of the open door to Becky's basement. That wasn't strong enough for Siegel. That's why we see the shadow of Becky's father before we see him coming out of the basement. When Miles sees his own shadow on the kitchen wall he connects the two images and that's what brings about his fear for Becky's welfare. But it confused people so they added Jack's line: "Miles, what about Becky? Do you think she's all right?"

DISSOLVE TO
EXT. BECKY'S HOUSE — FULL SHOT — NIGHT

Miles skids his car to a stop in front of the dark house and doesn't bother to set the brake. As he jumps out the car rolls forward and bumps the curb. Miles races across the lawn to the porch. He reaches out to ring the bell.

MILES: *(narration)* I was going to ring the bell then I had a hunch I'd better be careful. Something was wrong in this house.

He walks around to the side of the house to the basement window.

Note: The basement window is an add-on. The house may have had a basement, but if it did there wasn't a window where Siegel needed it. You can see the shadow cast on the black velveteen behind the glass.

Miles makes sure that nobody's watching then uses his elbow to break one of the panes of glass. Carefully he removes the broken pieces from the frame, then reaches in and unlocks the window.

INT. BASEMENT — FULL SHOT — NIGHT

Miles crawls through the window. He lights a match and searches the basement. He looks under the workbench. He opens a cupboard filled with empty mason jars and paint cans. The flame burns his fingers. He lights another match and throws the light around the room again. He crosses to a large wooden bin. He lifts the lid.

CLOSE ON NAKED BODY flat on its back, half covered by a blanket, an unfinished, underdeveloped, vague and indefinite Becky Driscoll.

Note: Siegel felt that the music in this sequence should be low and continue after Miles breaks the window to the time that he discovers the body of Becky in the box, at which point it should reach a high crescendo, similar to the way the music swelled when the audience first saw the body on the billiard table. For a change, Siegel got his wish. Carmen Dragon used exactly the same music for the moment when Becky's double is shown.

CLOSE SHOT — MILES eyes wide with horror. The match mercifully goes out. He lets the lid slam close and heads for the stairs.

INT. LOWER HALLWAY

Miles comes out of the basement and up the stairway to the second floor. He steps gingerly down the hall and opens the first door he comes to. Through the partly opened door we see Becky's father, asleep in his bed. Quietly, Miles closes the door and moves on to the next door.

INT. BECKY'S ROOM

Becky is in bed, asleep. Miles enters the moonlit room. He bends over her, shaking her shoulder.
MILES: *(sharply)* Becky. Becky.
She is deep in a drugged sleep. He shakes her again. Still she doesn't wake up. So he picks her up, snatches her robe from the foot of the bed, and carries her out of the room.

UP ANGLE STAIRWAY AND HALL

Miles, with Becky in his arms, makes his way down the stairs and out the front the door.

DISSOLVE TO
INT. MILES'S LIVING ROOM — NIGHT

Becky and Teddy are sitting on the sofa. Danny Kaufman sits across from them in a chair. Miles and Jack are standing.
JACK: Miles, would you tell me what happened?
MILES: The same thing. I found another one, coming to life in the cellar while I stood there watching it. It was Becky.
Teddy reacts and Becky puts her arm around her for comfort.

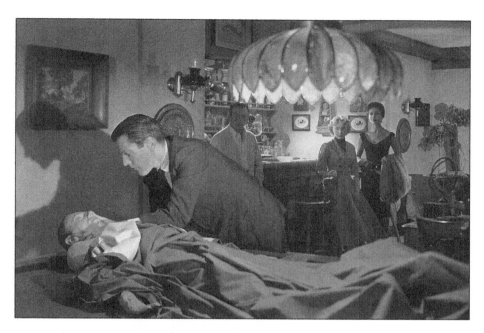

Above: While Jack, Teddy, and Becky watch, Miles examines the curious body that Jack found in his closet. Below: Miles finds Becky's double in the cellar of the Driscoll home.

Miles pulls Becky out of bed and carries her to safety.

DANNY: Yeah? I want to see one of these bodies.

MILES: All right.

DANNY: *(to Teddy)* Now you're going to bed. *(to Becky)* And you're staying with her. *(to Miles)* Put on your clothes. We'll go to Jack's first.

Jack gives Teddy a kiss and follows Miles out of the room.

DANNY: *(the last to leave)* You got any coffee around here?

MILES: *(o.s.)* Yeah, you'll find some in the kitchen.

TEDDY: He doesn't believe me, Beck.

BECKY: He will.

DISSOLVE TO

INT. BELICEC PLAYROOM — NIGHT

The door is open and the body is gone. Jack is the first one to reach the table and pointlessly flings the rubber sheet aside.

JACK: *(furious)* Somebody's playing games.

DANNY: Rough ones. *(points)* There's a blood spot.

Note: In the script, when Jack flings the rubber sheet aside, they find a pile of thick, grey fluff in place of the body. Jack picks up a handful of it and says, "And what's this stuff?" Danny dismisses it as ordinary dust but Miles picks up some of it and says, "It doesn't look ordinary to me. Feels like some type of vegetable matter. Fibrous..." Danny picks up some of it and puts it in his wallet. "If it makes you happy," he says to Miles, "I'll run a lab test on it." At the close of the scene, after the three walk out, a gust of wind blows the fluff from the table. Later, when the three of them go to Becky's house, they find another pile of dust in the bin where Miles saw Becky's double. In Finney's novel, the grey fluff is what becomes of the duplicates when the transformation is interrupted. In a letter to Allied Artists, written by William K. Everson (an early reader of the script for Allied Artists' foreign distributor), Everson said he thought the fluff would be difficult to film and too complex to follow. Apparently Siegel agreed because even though it was in the shooting script it was never filmed and all references to it were scratched.

DANNY: What you saw was the body of a murdered man. Did you examine it carefully?

MILES: Yes. It was not an ordinary body and there wasn't a mark on it.

JACK: I checked it too, when I put it on the table. There wasn't a scratch.

DANNY: You can kill a man by shoving an ice pick into the base of his brain, leaving a puncture so small the naked eye can't see it.

MILES: Danny, you're ignoring the fact that this was not a normal body. And you heard what Teddy said about the hand.

DANNY: I heard lots of things Teddy said and none of them made any sense.

JACK: All right now, hold on, pal, I was here too. So was Miles. *(pulls out the paper with the blank fingerprints)* Look at that. We took its fingerprints. Tell me why he didn't have any.

DANNY: He didn't want any so he took them off with acid.

JACK: *(hotly)* Stop trying to rationalize everything, will you. Let's face it, we have a mystery on our hands.

DANNY: Sure you have; a real one. Whose body was it and where is it now? A completely normal mystery. Whatever it is, it's well within the bounds of human experience and I don't think you ought to make any more of it.

MILES: Look, I wouldn't, if I hadn't looked in Becky's cellar. How do you explain away the body I saw there?

DANNY: I don't think you saw one there.

MILES: You don't think I saw one here, either?

DANNY: I know you did because three others saw it too.

MILES: But I dreamed up the second one.

DANNY: *(dryly)* Doctors can have hallucinations too. The mind is a strange and wonderful thing. I'm not sure it will ever figure itself out, everything else maybe, from the atom to the universe, everything except itself.

MILES: Nevertheless, I saw Becky's double, and the body we saw here bore an uncomfortable resemblance to Jack.

JACK: Mighty uncomfortable.

DANNY: All right. Let's go on to Becky's and have a look.

DISSOLVE TO

INT. BASEMENT — BECKY'S HOUSE — THREE SHOT — DANNY, JACK, AND MILES

They've already crawled through the window. Danny has a flashlight. *Note: His flashlight looks more like a flood light.*

DANNY: All right, where's your girlfriend's double?

MILES: *(points to the bin)* Okay, skeptic, lift the lid.

Danny crosses to the bin, opens the lid, and sweeps the light across the length of the box quickly then trains it on Jack and Miles.

DANNY: There's a body here all right.

MILES: It's Becky's double!

JACK: It sure is!

DANNY: Take another look.

They come forward. Danny throws the light into the wood bin. There's nothing but a blanket.

DANNY: Now you see it, now you don't.

MILES: *(stubbornly)* It was there, half-hidden by that blanket.

DANNY: You said you saw it there just now.

MILES: *(confused)* I thought I did.

DANNY: Why did you come here tonight? You'd seen a dead man at Jack's, an average sized man. The face in death was smooth and unlined, bland in expression, which often happens. You'd just become aware of a curious, unexplainable epidemic mass hysteria. Men, woman, and children suddenly convinced themselves that their relatives weren't their relatives at all. So your mind started playing tricks, and reality became unreality. The dead man became Jack's double in your eyes.

MILES: *(shakes his head)* Come off it, will you, Danny?

DANNY: I know, Miles, this is all hard to believe. But these things happen, even to witch doctors like me.

MILES: *(opens the lid again)* I saw her here. She was real.

DANNY: You saw her all right, in every tiny detail, as vividly as anyone has ever seen anything but only in your mind.

JACK: Look, Danny, you can talk all night but you're not going to convince me.

The basement is suddenly flooded with light. At the top of the stairs stands Becky's father, shotgun at ready.

BECKY'S FATHER: What in heaven's name are you doing in my cellar?!

DANNY: Using it for an office, Mr. Driscoll. These gentlemen are patients, badly in need of psychiatric treatment.

(o.s.) A police SIREN sounds.

BECKY'S FATHER: Oh, stop talking nonsense.

DANNY: I'm not. They've been having nightmare.

BECKY'S FATHER: Well, if you're drunk you'd better sober up quick. The police are on their way.

MILES: Oh no, no, no. We're not drunk.

DANNY: Nothing as simple as that. Pull up a chair.

BECKY'S FATHER: Why, you're crazy, all of you.

The Police Chief, NICK GRIVETT, is at the window, gun in hand.

NICK: Hey! What's going on down there?

Above: "I found another one. In the cellar of Becky's house, coming to life while I stood there watching it. It was Becky." Below: Becky's father (Kenneth Patterson), holding a shotgun, wants to know what in heaven's name these three men are doing in his cellar.

DANNY: Hello, Nick. Glad to see you. You saved these two characters a trip to the station. They want to report finding a body and losing it.

NICK: Where? When?

JACK: At my place, about seven o'clock.

NICK: Why'd you wait so long to report it? You know better than that, Doc.

MILES: Yeah, well, it was a curious sort of a body and then it wasn't there anymore.

NICK: I've got a good mind to throw you both in jail!

MILES: If you'd seen it, you'd understand why we waited.

NICK: Thin man, five ten, fingerprints burned off with acid? I just seen it on a slab in the morgue; turned up in a burning haystack on Mike Gessner's south pasture two hours ago. Now, break it up! Gone on home!

MILES: *(to Danny)* Well, you win. Pick up the marbles.

Everyone starts up the stairs.

DANNY: You pick 'em up. You need 'em more than I do.

FADE TO BLACK

FADE IN

INT. MILES' KITCHEN — MED. SHOT — MORNING

Becky, in one of Miles' shirts and a pair of his jeans, stands at the stove, making breakfast. The sleeves of the shirt are rolled up and the tail of it is tied around her slim waist. Miles walks in.

MILES: Good morning.

BECKY: *(smiling warmly)*: Good morning.

Before he can kiss her she hands him a glass of orange juice.

BECKY: Orange juice.

MILES: Thank you. *(sets in on the table)*

BECKY: How do you like your eggs?

MILES: Oh, any way you'd like them.

BECKY: Boiled? Two minutes?

MILES: Two minutes! Okay. *(takes her chin in his hand)* You know, dragging you out of bed in the middle of the night was a lot of trouble, but it was worth it.

BECKY: Seriously, Miles…

They hear a sound in the cellar. Miles flings open the door.

MILES: *(sharp)* Who is it?

DOWN ANGLE SHOT INTO CELLAR

From this angle we see only the portion of the cellar at the bottom of the short flight of stairs.

CHARLIE'S VOICE: *(o.s.)* Gas man.

With that a man moves into the shot. He is CHARLIE BUCHOLTZ, the gas meter reader.

CHARLIE: Morning, Doc.

MILES: *(sheepish)* Good morning, Charlie. I'm a little jittery. Not getting enough sleep.

CHARLIE: I won't be bothering you anymore. I'm putting a meter outside in the patio.

ANGLE ON MILES AND BECKY

She's standing beside him now.

MILES: Okay.

He tries to kiss her again but she scurries back to the stove.

BECKY: The eggs should be hard-boiled.

Miles takes a seat at the table.

MILES: Did you do this for your husband?

BECKY: Sure. Didn't your wife do it for you?

MILES: Oh, yes. She liked to cook. That's one of the reasons I'm single. I was never there when dinner was on the table. Well, take my advice and don't get mixed up with a doctor. They're seldom at home.

Becky sets a class of juice on the table and his boiled egg, and puts her arms around his neck.

BECKY: What if I told you I was already mixed up with a doctor?

MILES: *(holding her arms)* I'd say it was too good to be true.

BECKY: Things like this can happen all of a sudden.

MILES: What's all of a sudden about two people who have known each other most of their lives?

The door swings open and Jack walks in. Becky quickly returns to the stove and Miles pretends a sudden interest in his egg.

JACK: Good morning.

MILES: Oh, good morning.

JACK: I thought I smelled coffee. Why didn't you give me a call?

BECKY: I didn't want to wake Teddy.

JACK: Oh, she's wide awake. Got a good sleep.

MILES: Good.

JACK: But I don't feel she should go home right away, Miles. Would you mind taking in a couple of borders for a while? *(looking at Becky wisely)* Or did you have something else in mind?

MILES: *(glances at Becky)* I was toying with an idea but you can stay. Becky has filled a cup with coffee and hands it to Jack.

BECKY: Here, Jack.

JACK: Thanks, doll. I'll take it to Teddy.

Jack exits. **Becky sits at the table on Miles' right.**

MILES: **Don't you want to know what the idea is?**

BECKY: **Your breakfast's getting cold.**

MILES: **All right. But would you mind sitting over here at my left,** instead of my right?

BECKY: *(puzzled)* No, but why? *(she sits at his left.)*

MILES: *(smiles)* Because I kiss left-handed, if you know what I mean.

BECKY: *(smiling back)* No, I don't.

MILES: **Well, a girl at my right** *(curves his arm around the empty space at his right side)* **is uncomfortable for me. It just doesn't feel right somehow; it's something like trying to write with the wrong hand. I just don't kiss well, except to my left.**

He lifts his left arm around her shoulders and, meeting no resistance, kisses her.

BECKY: **Oh, a South Paw.**

DISSOLVE TO

EXT. WILMA'S ANTIQUE SHOP — MED. SHOT

The shop, a small one and typical, is in the middle of the block. Wilma is standing at the window with her arms folded. Miles' reflection can be seen in the glass. As he approaches Wilma moves away from the window and steps out on the sidewalk.

WILMA: Miles, did you make that appointment for me with the psychiatrist?

MILES: *(stopping)* Yes. Two o'clock.

WILMA: *(embarrassed)* I don't need him. I feel like such a fool. I woke up this morning and everything was all right. You don't know how relieved I am.

MILES: *(reassuringly touches her shoulder)* Oh, yes I do. Would you give Becky a call and tell her about it. She was worried about you.

WILMA: All right.

MILES: She's at my house.

Above: "There's a body here all right," Danny says but he's only fooling. Below: "Would you mind taking in a couple of borders for a while?" Jacks asks Miles. "Or did you have something else in mind?"

WILMA: *(surprised)* At your house. Why?

MILES: Well, it's a long story but she'll tell you all about it.

He moves on. Wilma watches him a moment then, turning, flips the card hanging in the door from "Open" to "Closed," and enters.

INT. WILMA'S ANTIQUE SHOP

She closes the door and locks it. Her demeanor completely changes from animated to zombie-like. There's a man sitting with his back to CAMERA.

WILMA: Becky's still at his house.

The man turns. It's Becky's father.

BECKY'S FATHER: All right.

DISSOLVE TO

INT. MILES' OFFICE — SALLY arranging flowers in front of a mirror. We can see Miles' reflection when he enters. He takes off his hat.

SALLY: Good morning.

MILES: Morning, Sally.

SALLY: Take a peek at what's in the reception room.

Miles moves to the door and parts the curtain. Jimmy Grimaldi and his mother are sitting on the couch, looking at a magazine.

JIMMY: Mother, why don't we go home?

ANNA: *(hugs him warmly)* In a little while, Jimmy.

Miles lets the curtain fall back into place. He walks away from the door, not sure what to make of these sudden one-eighty turns.

SALLY: He certainly made a quick recovery.

Miles goes to the window and stares at the town below.

MILES: I guess we all have.

DISSOLVE TO

EXT. MILES' CARPORT — NIGHT

Miles pulls to a stop.

MILES: *(narration)* But driving home I had a lot of questions and no answers. How could Jimmy and Wilma seem so normal now? Surely I had done nothing to cure them. Maybe they wanted me to feel secure but why?

Note: Siegel particularly wanted this bit of narration to go. He thought it was unnecessary but, then, isn't it all?

Miles gets out of his car with a package of meat in his hand. CAMERA PANS to the patio where Jack is trying to light the charcoal in the barbeque. Becky stands behind him mixing drinks.

MILES: Well!

BECKY: I hope you didn't forget the steaks.

Miles tosses the package to Jack.

MILES: I never forget anything.

TEDDY: *(coming out of the house)* Don't worry about him, he's completely housebroken.

JACK: I need a martini, Beck.

BECKY: Onion or olive?

JACK: It doesn't matter. I'm going to pour it on the charcoal. I can't get this stuff to burn.

MILES: *(carrying the martini to Jack)* Oh, a martini isn't dry enough. I'll get you something to start it. *(hands him the drink)* For drinking purposes. *(on his way to get the lighter fluid he encounters Teddy)* You're looking shipshape.

TEDDY: Thank you, sir. *(stuffs a potato chip into his mouth)*

INT. GREENHOUSE

The light is dim. On either side of the structure are wooden tables with rows of potted plants. In f.g. a pod-like object seems to be pulsating, splitting open, and white stuff is spilling out. In b.g. Miles grabs the lighter fluid which is on a shelf by the doorway and doesn't notice the strange objects until he returns the can to the shelf. He's on his way back out when hears a CRACKLE and POP. Now he sees them, four giant seed pods, pulsating and foaming. Miles stares at them in horrified unbelief.

MILES: *(crying out)* Jack! Jack!

Jack is there in a flash with Becky and Teddy close behind him. The four of them watch in horror as one by one they are being duplicated.

BECKY: They're like huge seed pods.

There's a pod for each of them. They split and white blanks pop out and slowly take form.

JACK: This must be the way the body in my closet was formed. Miles, where do they come from?

MILES: I don't know. If they are seeds or seed pods they must grow someplace, on a plant probably, and somebody or something wants this duplication to take place.

BECKY: But when they're finished what happens to our bodies?

Above: Miles, Teddy, and Becky watch Jack struggle with the barbeque. It is the calm before the storm. Below: Miles, Becky, Teddy, and Jack discover giant seed pods in Miles' greenhouse.

MILES: I don't know. When the process is completed probably the original is destroyed or disintegrates.

Jack turns suddenly and picks up a pitchfork. He starts toward the pods.

MILES: No! Wait!

JACK: Sorry but I take a dim view of watching my own destruction take place.

MILES: There isn't any danger until they're completely formed. We learned that last night at your house. Your blank didn't change right away.

TEDDY: (suddenly remembering) Not until you fell asleep.

JACK: **I have a feeling it'll be a long time before I sleep again.**

TEDDY: Miles, when the change does take place, do you suppose there's any difference?

MILES: There must be. Wilma noticed it. So did little Jimmy.

BECKY: (tearful) So did I. My father.

MILES: That must be what he was doing in the cellar last night, placing one of these. (holds her) I'm sorry.

BECKY: I felt something was wrong but I thought it was me because I've been away for so long.

TEDDY: They have to be destroyed — all of them!

MILES: They will be! Every one of them! (grabs Jack's shoulder) Listen, we have to search every building, every house in town. Men, women, and children are going to have to be examined. We've got some phoning to do.

Jack grimly holds onto his pitchfork.

JACK: I'm going to stay right here where I can watch them.

TEDDY: I'm going to stay with you.

Miles and Becky have just cleared the doorway when Jack stops them in their tracks.

JACK: And don't call the police! Nick Grivett didn't find anybody on a burning haystack!

EXT. GREENOUSE — MILES AND BECKY

Miles knows Jack's right. His mind is racing, wondering what to do. He slowly starts for the house.

BECKY: Why don't you call Danny? Maybe he can help.

Miles pauses for a moment.

MILES: Danny? No. I'm afraid it's too late to call Danny too.

BECKY: Well, what are you going to do?

MILES: Get help. (runs to the house) I hope whatever's taken place is confined to Santa Mira because if it isn't...

INT. MILES'S HOUSE — HALLWAY

Miles picks up the phone and dials the operator.

OPERATOR: *(filtered)* Operator.

MILES: Hello. This is Dr. Bennell. This is an emergency. I want to talk to the Federal Bureau of Investigation in Los Angeles.

BECKY: Can you make them believe you?

MILES: I've got to.

BECKY: Where do they come from?

MILES: *(begins pacing)* So much has been discovered these past few years that anything is possible. It may be the result of atomic radiation on plant life or animal life. Some weird alien organism. A mutation of some kind.

BECKY: But why should they take the form of people? Of us?

MILES: I don't know. I don't know. Whatever it is, whatever intelligence or instinct it is that can govern the forming of human flesh and blood out of thin air is…Well, it's fantastically powerful, beyond any comprehension, malignant. All that body in your cellar needed was a mind and it was…

BECKY: And it was taking mine while I was asleep. I could take that pitchfork myself and…

OPERATOR: *(filtered)* On your call to Los Angeles, Doctor. They don't answer.

MILES: *(sharp)* Well try again. That office is open day and night. *(puts his hand over the mouthpiece)* If they've taken over the telephone office we're dead.

INT. GREENHOUSE — JACK AND TEDDY

Jack still has the pitchfork. Teddy is clutching his shoulder.

ANGLE ON BLANK

As the foam evaporates we see the head and shoulders Teddy's double.

RETURN TO JACK AND TEDDY

TEDDY: Is that me?

Leaving Teddy, Jack slowly moves through the greenhouse, past each of the duplicates. When he comes to the last one he turns to Teddy.

JACK: **You've got good company, kid. We're all here.**

INT. MILES' HOUSE — HALLWAY — MILES AND BECKY

Miles is still on the phone only now he's yelling into the mouthpiece; his patience at an end.

MILES: This is an emergency, emergency! Now look, there's been... *(taps the receiver buttons)* Operator, get me a better connection.

OPERATOR: *(filtered)* I'll try, Doctor. *(pause)* It's no use. All of the Los Angeles circuits are dead.

MILES: All right, try Sacramento. Get me the state capital. I want to talk to the governor.

OPERATOR: *(filtered)* The Sacramento circuits are busy, Doctor. I'll call you back.

MILES: *(realizes it's hopeless)* All right. All right. I'll wait for your call. *(hangs up the phone)* I'll take the phone outside.

END OF REEL FOUR

EXT. PATIO — FULL SHOT

Miles and Becky run to the patio.

MILES: *(calling)* Jack!

He puts the phone on a table and, followed by Becky, crosses to meet Jack and Teddy as they come out of the greenhouse.

JACK: Yeah!

MILES: They've got the phones! Now you and the girls get in your car and make a run for it. First town you get to yell for help.

JACK: But what about you?

MILES: In a little while that phone's going to ring. If there's nobody here to answer it they'll know we've gone and block the roads out of town. I'll stall them until you're out of reach.

JACK: Well then what are you going to do?

MILES: Try and find out what's in back of this thing.

BECKY: I'm staying.

MILES: No!

BECKY: *(adamant)* Miles, don't ask me to leave you.

Miles looks at her steadily for a moment. He puts his arm around her.

MILES: Jack, get going.

JACK: Miles, I can't!

MILES: *(takes the pitchfork)* Look, somebody's got to go or we don't get any help.

TEDDY: Please, let's get out of here.

Above: "On your call to Los Angeles, Doctor. They don't answer." Below: "You and the girls get in your car and make a run for it. First town you get to, yell for help!"

JACK: Well watch out for yourselves.

MILES: *(to Becky)* Go over by the phone. Stay there. When it rings, call me.

Becky goes to the phone. Miles turns toward the greenhouse and braces himself for what he's about to do.

INT. GREENHOUSE

Miles enters, holding tight to the pitchfork. Slowly, he approaches the first duplicate. The hair is Becky's. The unlined face is Becky's. It's so much like Becky he isn't able to stab it, at least, for the moment. He moves to his own blank. He breaks out into a cold sweat as he contemplates destroying his vague double. He takes a deep breath, brings the pitchfork up, and plunges the tines down into his double. At the instant the fork enters the body.

FLASH CUT TO
EXT. PATIO — HUGE CLOSEUP — PHONE ON TABLE
RINGING. CAMERA PANS UP as Becky brings the receiver to her ear.

BECKY: Hello.

OPERATOR: *(filtered)* Is Dr. Bennell there?

BECKY: Yes, I'll get him.

OPERATOR: *(filtered)* Never mind. Just tell him the Sacramento circuits are still busy and ask him if he wants me to keep trying.

BECKY: All right. Hold on.

INT. GREENHOUSE — MILES

He's just stabbed the last of the duplicates.

BECKY: *(o.s.)* Miles! The circuits are still busy.

MILES: Well tell her to keep trying. Also try San Francisco and Washington.

He raises the pitchfork and fiercely, wildly, jabs one of the blanks again and again. Then, flinging the fork from him runs out.

EXT. GREENHOUSE

Miles grabs Becky.

MILES: We're getting out of here right now.

BECKY: Well where are we going?

The operator tells Becky that all of the lines are still busy.

MILES: Sally's.

He takes the phone off the hook as they race off. CAMERA MOVES IN on the phone. *(O.s.)* we HEAR Miles and Becky getting into the car and driving off.

OPERATOR: *(filtered)* We're still unable to get through to Los Angeles. Do you wish me to keep trying? Dr. Bennell? Dr. Bennell?

Note: Siegel was not happy with the way the greenhouse sequence was cut together. He always said you only shoot what you need so when you finish they can't screw it up too bad. He overshot this sequence and lived to regret it. In a letter to Walter Wanger, dated May 19, Siegel expressed his concerns. He felt that the lead up to the discovery of the pods was better the way Dick Heermance had cut it than the way he'd cut it. After that, however, he wasn't happy at all. Heermance eliminated a shot of a rake falling against one of the pods which Siegel liked. He thought there were too many CLOSEUPS of the pods and wanted more of the reverse angle on the four principals. He also complained that all of the TWO SHOTS of the pods were gone." He couldn't remember all the cuts but his overall impression wasn't good." If you don't like what Dick has now done — which I haven't seen — I suggest we go back to what we had," Siegel suggested.

In the movie, when Miles attempts to call for help are thwarted by the operator, he covers the mouthpiece, turns to Becky, and says, "If they've taken over the telephone office we're dead." The scene then cuts back to Jack and Teddy in the greenhouse. Siegel liked it better when it cut to a four shot of the duplicates before we see Jack and Teddy. He had filmed the pitchfork entering Miles' double two different ways. Heermance picked the one that Siegel liked least, which is the one that appears in the movie. There was another take that was a PAN SHOT of the pitchfork entering the body.

Siegel also felt it would be more effective if the pods were kept off camera until Miles actually sees them. His suggestions were, for the most part, ignored. The sound department did, however, have the noise of Mile's car engine starting up and taking off over the operator's voice on the telephone at the end of the sequence which Siegel suggested.

EXT. GAS STATION

Miles drives up beside the pumps.

MILES: *(narration)* I needed someone I could trust, and I figured Sally, my nurse, was my best bet. I decided to phone her to see if she was at home. Maybe they hadn't taken over the pay phones.

MILES: I'll try the pay phone. *(gets out of the car and calls out)* Hey, Mac!

Mac appears from behind the pumps.

MAC: Oh, hi, Doc. How are you?

MILES: Listen, will you give me a couple of gallons fast? I'm in a hurry.

MAC: Sure. *(calling)* Martha! Doc's in a hurry. Get the windshield, will you?

Miles ducks into the phone booth in b.g. and closes the door. Mac reaches through the driver's window.

MAC: *(to Becky)* I have to have the keys to open the gas tank.

MARTHA appears with her Windex, sprays the windshield on the passenger side, and languidly wipes the glass.

MARTHA: *(amiably)* Somebody sick out this way?

BECKY: There's been an accident.

MARTHA: Funny we haven't heard about it.

BECKY: Well, it just happened.

ANGLE ON PHONE BOOTH

Miles has the receiver pressed against his ear.

MILES: *(narration)* Before I could even get her number I saw Mac closing the trunk of my car. He could have been checking my spare tire, but I didn't think so.

Note: Siegel wanted to be sure that when the NARRATION starts in the TELEPHONE BOOTH, that MILES' HEAD was not facing the telephone mouthpiece, otherwise it would look like he was talking into the telephone. Siegel wanted the NARRATION to start later and continue OVER the shot as MILES runs back towards his car. Yet another request that fell on deaf ears.

FULL SHOT

Miles exits the phone booth and trots to his car.

MAC: *(to Becky)* That should do it.

BECKY: Thank you.

MILES: All set?

MAC: *(gives Miles the keys)* All set, Doc.

MILES: Fine, thanks. *(gets into car)* Put it on my bill, will you?

MAC: Sure, Doc.

Miles drives off. Martha walks away with her bottle of Windex. Shoving his hands into his pockets, Mac watches them disappear into the night.

MED. SHOT — CAR

It turns into an alley and skids to a stop.

BECKY: Well what's the matter?

Miles throws the door open, hurries to the rear of the car and yanks the trunk open. Becky joins him. There are two pods in the trunk. Hauling them out, he sets them on the ground, pulls a flare out of the trunk, and sets them on fire.

MILES: We have to make it to Sally's house.

Note: Another wild line.

Miles slams the trunk closed. He and Becky return to the car and speed off. Flames leap up in front of CAMERA.

Note: In an earlier draft of the script Miles and Becky try to get out of town and find the road blocked by the police. On their return Mac spots them and alerts the authorities.

INT. MILES' MOVING CAR — MILES AND BECKY *(PROCESS)*

Miles cuts the wheel sharply.

MILES: *(narration)* I wasn't sure now there was anyone I could trust, but I took a chance and drove to Sally's anyway.

EXT. SALLY'S BUNGALOW AND STREET — FULL SHOT

Two cars are parked in front of the modest bungalow. The lights of Miles' car swing around the corner. He drives past the cars and parks at the curb.

MILES: *(narration)* When I saw several cars parked in front of the house I decided to play it safe.

Becky starts to open her door and Miles stops her.

BECKY: What's wrong?

MILES: Probably nothing. But we're not going in there until I'm sure it's safe. Slide over under the wheel and get out of here fast if anyone shows up looking for us.

REVERSE ANGLE — FROM SALLY'S BUNGALOW

Miles cuts across the lawn and cautiously approaches the porch. The shade is drawn on the window so he gingerly climbs over the rail and,

Above: "Becky's still at his house," Wilma tells Becky's father. Below: Miles is about to set fire to the pods he found in the trunk of his car.

keeping low, moves to one of the side windows. He rises and the back of his head partially blocks out the room until he ducks down out of sight and we see what he saw. There's a group in the living room — Sally, her husband, MICKEY, Aunt Aleda, Wilma and Uncle Ira — all sitting quietly in chairs. Becky's father walks in with a seed pod. Miles rises back up to peer around the side of the window.

Note: As Miles approaches the window in the initial cut, he hears the sound of laughter which makes him think everything's okay. Pod people wouldn't be laughing. Sally (o.s.) says "Not so loud. I want the baby to get to sleep." It turns out that the laughter is from the radio. When they cut Sally's line they cut the need for the radio.

BECKY'S FATHER: Baby asleep yet, Sally?

SALLY: Not yet but she will be soon and there'll be no more tears.

BECKY'S FATHER: Shall I put this in her room?

SALLY: Yes, in her playpen. No wait. Maybe I'd better take it.

She rises to take the pod. In CLOSE f.g. Nick Grivett's hand enters the scene to drop on Miles' shoulder.

NICK: Why don't you go in, Miles? We've been waiting for you.

Miles swings around and instinctively slams Nick in the stomach, then clips him on the jaw. Nick crumples. Hearing the commotion, Uncle Ira runs to the window as Miles tears off across the lawn. Becky's father and Mickey are the first two out the door, followed by Wilma and her aunt. The men chase after him.

MILES: *(calling)* Becky, start the car quick!

She throws the passenger door open and he jumps inside. She steps on the gas and the car roars away.

DISSOLVE TO

EXT. POLICE CAR — CLOSE ON WINDOW

The car is empty. From the radio inside we HEAR an announcement.

DISPATCHER: *(filtered)* Attention all units! Attention all units! Apprehend and detain Dr. Miles Bennell and Becky Driscoll, now believed heading north in a black and white Ford sedan, license number 2X37796.

CAMERA PANS to THE HOT DOG SHOW, a brightly lit outdoor fast food joint. There are two cops at the counter who turn and quickly return to their car.

DISPATCHER: *(filtered)* All units designated as roadblocks move to your stations. It is urgent. These two persons must be detained and not permitted to leave Santa Mira.

As the car pulls away from the curb

DISSOLVE TO

MONTAGE OF POLICE CARS moving through the streets of Santa Mira, searching for Miles and Becky. Abandoned cars are searched. People are questioned. Through much of it we HEAR dispatcher's alert repeated o.s.

Note: This montage may or may not have have been filmed for the movie. Whether it was or wasn't, part of it found its way into Roger Corman's 1959 black comedy, A Bucket of Blood.

DISSOLVE TO

INT. MOVING CAR — MILES AND BECKY — *(PROCESS)*

MILES: We'll try to make it to my office. Cut in to that alley on the right.

EXT. STREET AND ALLEY

Miles' car enters the alley and comes toward CAMERA, then makes a sharp turn into a used car lot. Becky parks between two cars. Miles takes a price tag from one of the other cars and slaps it on the windshield of his car. He and Becky race off with police sirens wailing in b.g.

EXT. ALLEY — DOWN ANGLE — FROM STAIRS

Miles and Becky round the corner and climb the back stairs to his office. Miles cautiously opens the fire door. After making certain the hall is empty, he and Becky enter.

INT. BUILDING — HALL — MILES AND BECKY

As they approach his office they hug the wall. Miles peeks around the corner, sees the coast is clear and goes to his door. As he shoves the key into the lock they hear someone on the floor below. A light goes on and someone is coming up the stairs. Miles quickly opens the door and he and Becky duck into his office.

INT. MILES' OFFICE

Miles and Becky hide in Miles' walk-through closet.

INT. CLOSET — MILES AND BECKY

There's a small window on the door, about eye level, with a grille on it. Moonlight filters through it. They HEAR the door open and the light goes on. Miles and Becky crouch down, not daring to breathe. They hear FOOTSTEPS. The NIGHT WATCHMAN appears at the window. He takes a quick look and moves on. Footsteps cross the office and the light goes off. There is a pause before the hall door closes.

BECKY: *(almost a whisper)* Do you think he'll come back?

MILES: I don't think they'll check again before morning. By then Jack should be here with help.

REVERSE ANGLE ON DOOR

Miles and Becky peek through the grille, just to be on the safe side before coming out of the closet.

BECKY: What if Jack doesn't get through?

Miles goes to the medicine cabinet and takes out a bottle of pills.

MILES: He's got to get through. *(hands her a couple of the pills)* Here, now take two of these. They'll help you to stay awake.

Miles pops a couple of pills into his mouth and goes to the water cooler. He and Becky fill paper cups with water to wash down the pills. Miles goes to the window and Becky follows.

MILES: We can't close our eyes all night.

BECKY: Or we'll wake up changed?

Miles nods grimly.

BECKY: To something evil and inhuman.

Note: Miles folds his arms when he says, "We can't close our eyes all night." After Becky joins him at the window the scene cuts to a closer angle and he folds his arms again. Either the continuity person was asleep or something was cut out in-between.

MILES: In my practice I've seen how people have allowed they're humanity to drain away. Only it happened slowly instead of all at once. They didn't seem to mind.

BECKY: Just some people, Miles.

MILES: All of us, a little bit. We harden our hearts, grow callous. Only when we have to fight to stay human do we realize how precious it is to us. How dear. As you are to me.

They kiss.

FADE TO BLACK

FADE IN

INT. MILES' OFFICE — CLOSE ON PHONE — DAY

As we FADE IN the phone RINGS. There an ashtray full of cigarette butts beside the phone. CAMERA PULLS BACK to include Miles and Becky sitting at the desk.

BECKY: Maybe that's Jack trying to find us.

MILES: He'd know better than to use the phones. *(intense)* Where is he? Why doesn't he come?

He squashes out his cigarette and goes to the window. He peers cautiously out.

MILES P.O.V. — THE SQUARE — DAY

People are driving up and parking their cars. Pedestrians move up and down the streets. Little knots of men and woman stand talking in entryways. Everything seems normal, peaceful — a small town getting ready for a big day.

INT. MILES' OFFICE — CLOSE SHOT —

MILES watching the activity.

MILES: *(softly)* Just like any Saturday morning.

Becky rises from her chair and joins him at the window.

MILES: Len Pearlman. Bill Bittner. Jim Clark, his wife, Shirley, and their kids; people I've known all my life.

BECKY: What time is it?

MILES: *(checks his watch)* Seven forty-five. Yeah, I know. It's too early to be so busy.

BECKY: What are they doing here?

HIGH ANGLE P.O.V. SHOT FEATURING BUS STOP

A Greyhound bus parks at the bus stop. Three passengers get off and are met by two policemen who hustle them into a police car.

MILES: *(o.s.)* There's the answer. Must be strangers in town.

They're waiting for the bus to come and go. There isn't another one through here until eleven.

With siren blaring the police car takes the strangers away.

Note: When the people get off the bus and the police hustle them into the police car, Dick Heermance cut the line: "They must be strangers in town." Siegel complained and the line was restored.

INT. MILES' OFFICE — CLOSE SHOT — MILES AND BECKY

The telephone RINGS and mixes with the sound of the SIREN. Miles and Becky both look at the phone but don't answer it. They turn back to the window.

LONG HIGH ANGLE P.O.V. SHOT — THE SQUARE

Another police car pulls up to the center of the square. The Police Chief, Nick Grivett, gets out and crosses to the platform in the center of the square. From all points, and all at once, the citizens of Santa Mira, in an orderly fashion, march to the square. Three large trucks pull up from three different directions and park in a semi-circle.

Note: After GRIVETT crossed to the platform in the square, Heermance tried to CUT to GRIVETT'S CLOSE SHOT and then to the LONG SHOT of the trucks entering the square. It didn't work. He tried to use a CLOSE SHOT of the truck entering instead but that didn't work either. There were more shots of the townspeople putting pods into their cars, most of which were eliminated. Only two cuts remained. In the final cut, Grivett walks toward the platform in a far shot, mounts the platform in a slightly closer shot, and the trucks enter in a far shot. The first close-up of the trucks comes when the tarpaulins are pulled away to reveal the pods.

MILES: *(o.s.)* Farmers — Grimaldi — Pixley — Gessner.

Each truck carries a load covered with canvas tarpaulins. The farmers pull the tarpaulins away. All three trucks are full of the horrible pods. Speaking into a megaphone, the police chief addresses the crowd.

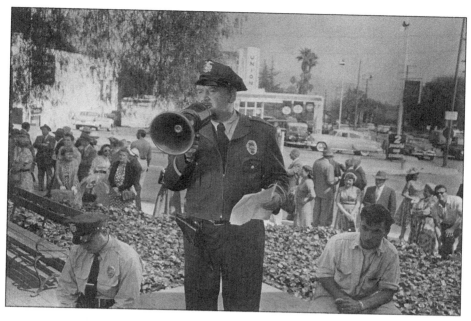

Above: Nick Grivett (Ralph Dumke) instructs the pod people which truck to go
to for their pods. Below: Farmers bring their pods to the center of town.

NICK: Crescent City — if you have Crescent City families, step over to truck number one. Crescent City: first truck.

Some of the people move to the rear of the first truck to receive their pods.

NICK: Redbank. All with Redbank families and contacts, go to truck number two. All with Redbank families and contacts, go to truck number two. Havenhurst: the first truck. Havenhurst: the first truck. Milltown: the third truck. Milltown: the third truck. Valley Springs.

People are crossing from the square to the trucks, picking up the pods and taking them to their cars. They open the trunks of their cars and put the pods inside, or carefully place them in the back seats. It is all very orderly, the whole operation being carried out with neatness and dispatch.

INT. MILES' OFFICE — CLOSE SHOT — MILES AND BECKY

MILES: First our town, then all the towns around us. It's a malignant disease spreading through the whole country.

NICK: (o.s.) That's all for today.

THE SQUARE — CLOSER ANGLE ON GRIVETT

NICK: Be ready again tomorrow.

He hands the megaphone to another officer and folds his list of towns. The crowd is dispersing. Cars are backing out and driving off. The empty trucks are pulling out. Without seeming to hurry, the people clear the square as if by magic.

INT. MILES' OFFICE — MILES AND BECKY

Miles quickly takes the small vial of pills from his pocket.

MILES: I can't wait for Jack any longer. (hands her the pills) Stay here.

BECKY: But you're not going out there?!

MILES: I've got to stop them!

BECKY: But wait, we're safe here!

As he turns toward the door he sees that someone is jiggling the knob. The two of them freeze.

JACK: (o.s.) They're not here! I hope we're not too late.

MILES: Jack — thank God!

Miles goes to the door, unlocks it, flings it open, and drags Jack by his arm into the room.

MILES: Jack, the whole town's been taken over by the pods.
Danny walks in.
DANNY: Not quite. There's still you and Becky.
Fear replaces Miles' expression of relief. He backs away from them.
DANNY: Miles, it would have been so much easier if you had gone to
sleep last night.
Danny goes to the window. Jack slowly approaches Miles and Becky
who back away.
JACK: Now relax. We're here to help you.
Instinctively, without taking his eyes off Jack, Miles lifts the phone
off the hook.
DANNY: You know better than that.
Grimaldi, one of the farmers, enters with Nick Grivett.
GRIMALDI: Where do you want us to put 'em?
DANNY: *(pleasantly)* Would you like to watch them grow?
MILES: *(bitterly)* No, thanks.
DANNY: *(indicating the Reception Room)* Put them in there. *(to Miles
and Becky)* There's nothing to be afraid of. We're not going to hurt you.
JACK: Look, once you understand you'll be grateful. Remember how
Teddy and I fought against it? Well, we were wrong.
Grimaldi and another man carry two pods into the Reception Room.
BECKY: You mean Teddy doesn't mind?
JACK: Of course not. She feels exactly the way I do.

*Note: This is one of my favorite lines. Teddy feels exactly the way he does
which is not at all.*

BECKY: *(desperately)* Let us go!
MILES: Look, we'll leave town. We won't come back.
DANNY: We can't let you go. You're dangerous to us.
JACK: Don't fight it, Miles, it's no use. Sooner or later you'll have to
go to sleep.
Grimaldi and the other man exit the room.
NICK: I'll wait for you in the hall.
Nick walks out and closes the door behind him. Danny steps away
from the window and removes his hat.
DANNY: Miles, you and I are scientific men. You can understand the
wonder of what's happened here. Now just think, less than a month ago
Santa Mira was like any other town; people with nothing but problems.
Then out of the sky came a solution. Seeds drifting through space for years

took root in a farmer's field. From the seeds came pods which have the power to reproduce themselves in the exact likeness of any form of life.

MILES: *(musing)* So that's how it began — out of the sky.

DANNY: Your new bodies are growing in there. They're taking you over, cell for cell, atom for atom. There's no pain. Suddenly, while you're asleep, they'll absorb your minds, your memories, and you're reborn into an untroubled world.

MILES: Where everyone's the same?

DANNY: Exactly.

MILES: What a world. We're not the last humans left. *(defiantly)* They'll destroy you.

DANNY: *(simply)* Tomorrow you won't want them to. Tomorrow you'll be one of us.

Miles draws Becky closer to him.

MILES: I love Becky. Tomorrow will I feel the same?

DANNY: There's no need for love.

MILES: No emotion. *(fiercely)* Then you have no feelings, only the instinct to survive. You can't love or be loved, am I right?

DANNY: You say it as if it were terrible. Believe me, it isn't. You've been in love before. It didn't last. It never does. Love, desire, ambition, faith — without them life's so simple, believe me.

MILES: I don't want any part of it.

DANNY: You're forgetting something, Miles.

MILES: What's that?

DANNY: You have no choice.

MILES: *(turning to Becky)* I guess we haven't any choice.

DANNY: Good.

Danny and Jack retire to the Reception Room and close the door.

BECKY: *(sobbing)* I want to love and be loved.

Miles kisses her.

BECKY: I want your children. I don't want a world without love or grief or beauty. I'd rather die.

MILES: No. No. Not unless there's no other way.

BECKY: Why didn't they just give us a shot or a sleeping pill or something?

He's only half listening to her now as he goes to the medicine cabinet, trying to think of some way to escape.

MILES: *(absently)* Drugs dull the mind. Maybe that's the reason. *(opens the cabinet and takes out three knives)* No. It wouldn't work. I might get one, maybe two, but I couldn't possible get three of them.

BECKY: You're forgetting something, darling — me. It isn't three against one, it's three against two. *(reaches out)* Give me a knife.

He considers her offer.

MILES: No.

He returns the knives to the cabinet and pauses for a moment. He takes a small bottle from the cabinet and shows it to Becky. She starts to ask what he's up to but he touches her to shush her. Mindful not to make any noise, he creeps to the hall door and locks it. He goes to the Reception Room.

CLOSE ON RECEPTION ROOM DOOR

Miles pulls the curtain back at the corner and we see Danny and Jack staring at the floor, watching the pods take form.

BACK TO MILES

He carefully slides the lock on the door. He begins loading hypodermic syringes with morphine.

END OF REEL FIVE

Becky watches in silence. When Miles is finished he hands one of the three syringes to her.

MILES: *(almost a whisper)* Go over by the desk.

He opens the door to his walk-through closet, the one he and Becky hid in earlier, kicks a medical table across the room, steps into the closet, and slams the door.

INT. RECEPTION ROOM — DANNY AND JACK

They go to the door and find it locked.

DANNY: What's going on in there?

JACK: It's locked.

DANNY: Miles! Miles!

JACK: What's going on, Miles?

DANNY: Unlock the door!

JACK: Miles. Open the door.

DANNY: Open the door, Miles!

JACK: Miles!

Miles comes out of the closet and stabs the two men in the back.

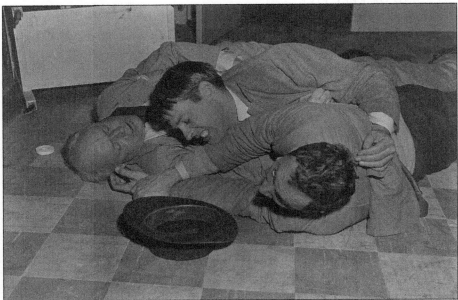

Above: Becky and Miles are told that there's no need for love in the world of the pod people. Below: Miles tries to hold Danny and Jack at bay until the morphine can take effect.

REVERSE ANGLE ON DOOR

The three men come crashing through and hit the floor.

INT. HALLWAY — NICK GRIVETT

Hearing the commotion he tries the door.
NICK: Open the door!

INT. MILES' OFFICE — ANGLE ON STRUGGLE

Jack and Danny kick and flail but Miles is able to hold them down until they succumb to the drug. The door bursts open and Nick rushes in. He delivers a judo chop that renders Miles helpless. Nick grabs him by the neck and starts to strangle him. Becky comes up behind Nick and plunges the needle into his neck. Nick releases his hold on Miles and turns on Becky. He reaches out for her but his legs give way and he hits the floor.
MILES: Our only hope is to make it to the highway.

Note: He actually says "freeway" but the freeway system wasn't running through the whole country yet and they thought some people might not know what a freeway was. So they changed it to "highway" in the dubbing.

INT. HALLWAY — FULL SHOT

Miles and Becky come out of his office. They stop at the turn and peer around before running down the hall to the rear fire door. It is padlocked.
MILES: *(grimly)* Well, that does it. The only other way is out the front door and there's bound to be somebody watching. *(shrugs)* We'll have to chance it.
They run back the way they came.

ANGLE ON STAIRWELL

Miles and Becky come racing around the corner.
MILES: Keep your eyes a little wide and blank. Show no interest or excitement.
As they scurry down the stairs they make an effort to straighten their rumbled clothes and mussed hair. As they hit the last few steps they slow down and calmly step out into the street.

EXT. MILES' OFFICE BUILDING —
FULL SHOT TOWARD ENTRANCE

There are people moving up and down the street past the building. Parked near the entrance is a police car. Janzek, the cop, is waiting outside. Miles and Becky walk up to him.

MILES: *(dully)* Well, Sam, we're finally with you.

JANZEK: They were supposed to let me know. The Chief said he'd phone the station, then I'd get the call.

MILES: He phoned but the line was busy. He's calling again now.

They walk on. Janzek suspiciously watches after them. A big truck passes by.

MED. SHOT — STREET — TRUCK AND DOG

A dog moves into the street in front of the truck. The truck slams on the brakes.

Note from Siegel to Wanger: The dog is seen scurrying past the truck which is actually better than my trying to kill the dog.

MED. SHOT — MILES AND BECKY

BECKY: *(screaming)* Look out!

CLOSE SHOT — JANZEK

He looks at Miles and Becky, puzzled.

MED. SHOT — MILES AND BECKY

Becky realizes she's betrayed herself.

BECKY: *(softly)* I'm sorry, Miles.

He takes her arm and they move on at the same deliberate pace. As they start across the street, Miles glances over his shoulder at Janzek.

CLOSE SHOT — JANZEK

Better safe than sorry, he turns and heads for Miles' office.

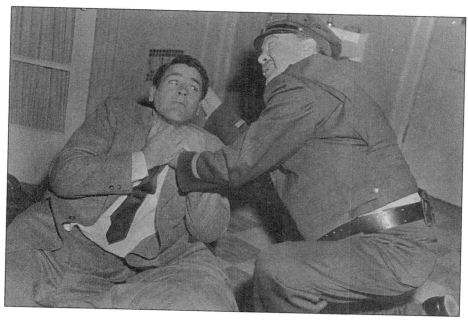

Above: Officer Grivett tries to subdue Miles with a judo chop. Below: Pretending to be pod people, Becky sees that a dog is about to be run over by a truck and her concern blows their cover.

INT. MILES' OFFICE BUILDING —
ANGLE ON STAIRS — JANZEK

He climbs the stairs. CAMERA PANS with him until he reaches the top then follows his action through the space between two slats in the stair rail. He startles when he looks through the open door to Miles' office.

Note: One of the slats has been removed from the railing to give the camera a better view. The actor also has to hug the rail a little bit to get past the camera.

EXT. STREET — MILES AND BECKY

They've dropped all pretenses now and are running full throttle up the street.

INT. MILES' OFFICE BUILDING — JANZEK

He hurries down the stairs.

EXT. MILES' OFFICE BUILDING — MED SHOT FROM POLICE CAR

Janzek steps out of the building and moves quickly to his car. He takes hold of the mike.
JANZEK: This is Janzek. They got away. Turn the main siren on.

THE CHASE
Miles and Becky approach a long stairway at a dead run. An air raid siren wails. It's an arduous climb up the very steep stairs. When they reach the top they're worn out and gasping for breath. Weakly, they stagger across the street and disappear over the brow of the hill.

Janzek leads the vanguard of the mob in pursuit. Before long a moving line of men and women extends up the stairway, almost to the top.

Miles and Becky plunge down a steep slope into a ravine. Miles, holding Becky's hand, pulls her up the brush-covered slope. They disappear over the crest with the mob not far behind.

Note from Siegel to Wanger: During the chase, I would like a SHOT of several of the pursuers before we see BECKY and MILES going under the tree and up the steep hill. If we follow the cut of Becky and Miles coming down the hill and immediately cut to them going up the hill we geographically narrow the chase.

Above: Miles and Becky run up what Kevin McCarthy called "those long, interminable stairs." Below: The pod people race toward the stairs.

Then I would like one shot of the pursuers scrambling to the top of the hill just before Miles sees the excavation in the tunnel. I think Dick is going to do this. What I did wrong before was to cut too many times to the pursuers coming up the hill.

EXT. TUNNEL ENTRANCE — FULL SHOT

Miles is pulling Becky after him when she stumbles, dropping her sweater in the process. He scoops her into his arms and carries her into the tunnel.

INT. TUNNEL — LONG SHOT TOWARD ENTRANCE

Miles carries her about ten feet into the tunnel and puts her back on her feet. They stagger a little further on, using the wall for support.
BECKY: *(shaking her head)* I can't! I can't! Miles, I can't! I can't go on!
MILES: Yes, you can.
He gives her a little push, puts his arm around her waist and together they move further on to a shored up section of tunnel. Here water drips from the ceiling, supported by heavy timbers. Miles looks desperately around for a place to hide and spots a gap between two of the boards that cover an excavation in the floor. He drops down on his hands and knees for a closer look. There's enough space in the ditch beneath the boards for them to hide. Miles shoves one large beam aside and lifts one of the boards to make enough room for them. They climb in. Miles gently eases Becky down on the wet earth and then replaces the boards as best he can. We hear the babble of the mob as they come closer to the cave.
JANZEK: This is her sweater. They must be in the tunnel.
Janzek leads the mob into the tunnel.
JANZEK: *(points)* Some of you go that way.

ANGLE PAST MILES AND BECKY

Through the cracks in the boards hurrying feet cross overhead.

MED. SHOT — CHARLIE BUCKHOLTZ

The gas meter man stops for a moment on the planks.
CHARLIE: *(yelling)* Give up! You can't get away from us. We're not going to hurt you. *(he runs on)* Give up.
END OF REEL SIX

Above: With Sam Janzek (Guy Way) in the lead, the pod people chase after Miles and Becky. Below: Exhausted, Miles and Becky want to know which direction will lead them to safety.

CLOSE UP — MILES AND BECKY

The sounds of tramping feet echo and re-echo through the tunnels and Miles and Becky draw even closer together.

JANZEK: *(o.s.)* They're not in the tunnel. All right, everybody outside. Come on. Check the hills. Everybody move.

DISSOLVE TO
INT. TUNNEL NEAR EXIT — NIGHT —
CLOSE DOWN ANGLE SHOT — SMALL POOL OF WATER

Moonlight coming through the tunnel exit illuminates the scene. Water drips steadily into the pool. There is no other sound but that of the dripping water. Then, as Miles' cupped hands enter the pool, CAMERA PULLS BACK and TILTS UP to reveal Miles and Becky kneeling by the pool. They splash water on their faces to keep themselves awake.

BECKY: *(resting her head on his shoulder)* I can't stay awake much longer.

MILES: I think they're all gone now. We'd better start or we'll never make it to the highway.

Note: Again, the line had to be dubbed because he said freeway.

As he helps her to her feet they hear the chords of a guitar and a woman wordlessly singing a beautiful melody. They follow the sound to an exit at the rear of the tunnel.

Note: Siegel was worried that the audience might think the music was part of the score. He suggested that it be "futzed" so that it would sound like it was coming from a car radio, which is exactly where it was supposed to be coming from. Siegel may have been getting a little punchy. Since Miles and Becky react to the music, it isn't likely that the audience would confuse it with scoring music. In the script, they hear a soft Mexican voice singing a Mexican song. Miles translates some of the lyrics for Becky. Carmen Dragon decided to use a melody his father, Frank, had composed one afternoon while he was strumming on his guitar. The woman singing the melody is Carmen Dragon's wife, Eloise.

BECKY: Miles, I've never heard anything so beautiful. It means we're not the only ones left who know what love is.

MILES: Stay here and pray they're as human as they sound. Bye, Darling.

Above: Miles carries Becky into the cave. Below: "Miles, I can't, I can't, I can't, I can't go on," Becky tells Miles.

Miles goes off to follow the music, hoping to find people that will help them to escape. Becky wearily goes back to the pool to splash more water on her face.

EXT. HILLSIDE — MED. SHOT — MILES

Miles, finding the going easier now the hill has leveled off a little, goes through the brush.

EXT. HILLSIDE NEAR TOP — MILES

He moves cautiously now.

FULL SHOT — GREENHOUSES AND WORKERS — MILES' P.O.V.

A row of long greenhouses gleams in the moonlight. Workers are taking the pods and loading them into a truck. The MUSIC comes to an end.

DISC JOCKEY: (filtered) This is station KCAA, the twenty-four hour platter parade, the station of music...

Somebody turns off the radio.

EXT. HILL TOP — CLOSE UP — MILES

He's too exhausted to register much disappointment. Keeping low, he goes back the way he came.

Note: To make the shot a little more interesting, there's a tree branch entering the left side of the frame, obviously being held by someone.

EXT. HILLSIDE — MILES moving through the brush.

FULL SHOT — MOUTH OF TUNNEL AND HILLSIDE

Miles stumbles down the last step ditch and turns toward the tunnel.

INT. TUNNEL — FULL SHOT — MILES

He expected to find Becky waiting for him.

MILES: Becky! Becky! Becky! Where are you?

BECKY: (o.s.) I'm here, Miles.

Miles finds her lying down in the middle of the tunnel. He lifts her up.

Above: Sam Janzek, with Becky's sweater in his hand, tells the pod posse to
spread out. Below: Miles and Becky fight to stay awake.

MILES: You didn't go to sleep?

BECKY: I'm so tired.

MILES: They weren't people. It was more of them. They're growing thousands of pods in greenhouses. We've got to get away.

BECKY: I'm exhausted Miles, I can't make it.

He picks her up in his arms and carries her. As he reaches the entrance he stumbles and they fall into a puddle of water. While he catches his breath he kisses her neck and cheek.

BECKY: We can't make it without sleep.

MILES: Yes we can.

He kisses her on the lips, then slowly pulls himself away. He looks at her in horror.

BECKY: (firmly) I went to sleep, Miles, and it happened.

MILES: Oh, Becky.

BECKY: (rising up) They were right.

MILES: I should never have left you.

BECKY: Stop acting like a fool, Miles, and accept us.

MILES: (shakes his head) No. Never!

Becky looks at him steadily then shouts.

BECKY: He's in here!

Miles scrambles to his feet and runs off.

BECKY: Get him! Get him!

Becky goes to the mouth of the tunnel and watches him disappear into the night.

EXT. ANGLE ON HILLSIDE — FAR SHOT

Miles stumbles down a steep ravine with a small group of the pod people on his heels. Half-blind with fatigue and exertion, Miles half-rolls, half-falls down the slope.

MILES: (narration) I've been afraid a lot of times in my life, but I didn't know the real meaning of fear until…until I kissed Becky. A moment's sleep and the girl I loved was an inhuman enemy bent on my destruction. That moment's sleep was death to Becky's soul, just as it had been for Jack and Teddy and Dan Kauffman and all the rest. Their bodies were now hosts harboring an alien form of life. A cosmic form, which to survive must take over every human man. So I ran. I ran. I ran as little Jimmy Grimaldi had run the other day. My only hope was to get away from Santa Mira and get to the highway, to warn the others of what was happening.

Above: Miles and Becky work their way to the back entrance of the cave, hoping to find the source of the beautiful music. Below: "Stay here and pray they're as human as they sound."

Note: Since Steve Broidy was so concerned about mixing humor with horror, they should have done something about the line "I didn't know the real meaning of fear until I kissed Becky." It's always gotten big laughs every time I've seen the film with an audience. Siegel wanted it cut.

He also wanted Heermance to restore a scene of MILES falling down in the ROAD during the chase. He didn't.

Miles stumbles down to a road and runs toward a bridge which crosses the Freeway. The pod people, led by Janzek, are hot on his heels. Charlie Bucholtz stops them.

CHARLIE: Wait!

JANZEK: No! No! We've gotta get him!

CHARLIE: Let him go. They'll never believe him.

Note: In response to a questionnaire Siegel wrote, "All of the shots on the highway of Kevin trying to stop traffic were shot on a cross bridge across the Hollywood Freeway. This particular bridge was not used by much normal traffic. We cordoned it off and shot from daybreak to dawn, completing all our work. There was no second unit on this sequence or, for that matter, nowhere else in the picture. There was no process used at all or any other trick mediums during this sequence."

LONG SHOT FROM THE POD PEOPLES' P.O.V. — MILES as he stumbles into the middle of the Freeway Bridge.

MILES: Help! Help! Help! Wait!

MED. SHOT — MILES standing in the middle of the bridge, exhausted, unshaven, and dirty. Cars pass by, so close to him that they look as if they're going to hit him. He puts his hands on the cars as if he hoped to stop them.

MILES: Wait! Wait! Stop! Stop and listen to me! *(stands directly in front of a car)* Listen to me!

The driver slams on the brakes. Miles goes to the window.

MILES: Listen. Listen. Those people are coming after me. They're not human.

The driver moves on. Miles goes to the next car.

MILES: Listen to me! We're in danger! Please!

Every now and then a driver will give vent as Miles continues to dodge in and out of the traffic, begging people to listen to him.

Above: To his dismay, Miles sees where the music is coming from. Below: As farmers load pods onto their truck, a radio disc jockey says, "This is station KCAA, the twenty-four hour platter parade."

MILES: There isn't a human being left in Santa Mira!

He jumps on the running board of a truck.

MILES: Hey, stop! Pull up, will you? Pull over to the side of the road. I need your help. Something terrible has happened!

DRIVER: *(pushes him off)* Go on, your drunk. Get outta the street. Get outta here!

Miles falls against the truck and spins with the movement as it passes by. Painted on the canvas, in bold letters, are the names of the cities that mark the truck's destination: LOS ANGELES, SAN FRANCISCO, PORT-LAND and SEATTLE. Miles chases after the truck and jumps onto the back of it. To his horror he sees that the truck is full of pods. He jumps back off and is nearly hit by a car.

DRIVER: What, are you crazy, you big idiot.

MILES: Look, you fools, you're in danger? Can't you see? They're after you! They're after all of us! Our wives! Our children! Everyone! *They're here already! You're next!*

Note: The script has a slightly different finale. For one thing, it doesn't have the chilling bit with the truck. Instead, Miles comes to the window of a middle-aged woman who is watching him with horror and fascination. "Get help!" he tells her. She rolls up her window. He pleads with her until he falls to the ground from exhaustion. Cars surround him. The woman, with sympathy, asks, "Is he ill — was he hit?" Half delirious, Miles rambles on. "Go wherever they are — kill them! Find the field where they grow…" he says as two or three men gently lift him up into a closeup, "…and burn them. Burn them! There's no escape — no time to waste…Unless you do, you'll be next."

DISSOLVE TO

INT. DOCTOR'S OFFICE — EMERGENCY HOSPITAL — NIGHT

Miles sits on the couch between the two doctors.

MILES: *(after studying their faces)* You don't believe a word of this, do you? Sure it's fantastic but it happened? Don't just sit there measuring me for a straitjacket. Do something! Get on the phone! Call for help!

When no one moves to do that, Miles buries his face in his hands.

MILES: Oh, what's the use?

Bassett and Hill step back out into the hall, closing the door behind them.

DR. BASSETT: Well, what do you think? Will psychiatry help?

DR. HILL: If all this is a nightmare, yes.

Above: The kiss that betrays Becky. Below: "He's in here! He's in here! Get him! Get him!"

DR. BASSETT: Of course it's a nightmare. Plants from another world taking over human beings — mad as a March hare.

An intern, accompanied by an ambulance driver, rolls an injured man into the hall.

DR. BASSETT: What have we here?

AMBULANCE DRIVER: Ran his truck through a red light. Greyhound bus smacked him broadside and tipped him over.

DR. BASSETT: *(to the intern)* Put him in the o.r.

The intern continues on down the hall.

DR. BASSETT: Would you take over Bennell for me, Doctor?

DR. HILL: Certainly.

DR. BASSETT: *(to driver)* How badly was he hurt?

AMBULANCE DRIVER: Both legs, left arm broken all to bits. We had to dig him out of the most peculiar things I ever saw.

Dr. Hill has just opened the door to the room where Miles is waiting.

DR. HILL: What things?

Miles gets off the couch and comes to the door.

AMBULANCE DRIVER: I don't know what they are. I never saw them before. They looked like great big seed pods.

DR. BASSETT: Seed pods?

DR. HILL: *(urgently)* Where was the truck coming from?

AMBULANCE DRIVER: Santa Mira.

Dr. Hill looks at Miles who nods. At that Dr. Hill goes hurriedly into the office and addresses the two officers who were guarding Miles.

DR. HILL: Get on your radio and sound an all points alarm. Block all highways and stop all traffic and call every law enforcement agency in the state.

CAMERA follows the two officers as they leave the office and comes to rest on Miles, leaning against the wall, exhausted but, at last, vindicated.

DR. HILL: *(o.s.)* Operator, get me the Federal Bureau of Investigation. Yes, it's an emergency!

Note from Siegel to Wanger: After MILES says "Thank God!" it is not necessary that we hear too clearly the offstage lines of DR. HILL getting the Operator and asking for the F.B.I. The MUSIC should star to swell up following the "Thank God!" [It's Miles saying "Thank God!" that we don't hear. Dr. Hill comes through loud and clear.]

FADE TO BLACK

Above: Officer Janzek wants to go after Miles but Charlie Bucholtz (Sam Peckinpah) tells him to wait. "Let him go. They'll never believe him." Below: Miles runs into the middle of traffic to warn the people of the impending threat.

CHAPTER EIGHT

PROMOTION AND PUBLICITY

Steve Broidy may not have been able to convince anyone that his title *They Came from Another World* was the be all and end all, but it managed to work its way into the ad campaign. Check out this copy from the opening day:

> "THEY COME FROM ANOTHER WORLD! While the earth sleeps IT happens! The creeping mass of doom engulfs entire town! Incredible, insatiable cosmic hordes take over every living human! Never has the screen erupted into so monstrous a nightmare of terror!"

The mogul must have really thought he had something. Or maybe he was just weenie wagging.

The Body Snatchers was released without much fanfare on February 5, 1956. Walter Wanger hoped that the studio would open the picture in one or two theaters as a single attraction so the public would understand it was something special, giving it time to build an audience. But the film was given no special treatment. It was thrown into general release with an undistinguished British sci-fi film, *The Atomic Man*.

These days most films open nationwide. In the old days they went from city to city. New York was often the premiere city, as it was for *The Body Snatchers*. But, the picture wasn't booked into one of the Big Apple's Broadway theaters. It opened in Brooklyn at the Albee.

To promote the picture Allied Artists relied on the usual bag of tricks: trailers, posters, and newspaper ads.

When Don Siegel shot the frame story, he filmed an additional close-up of Kevin McCarthy for the trailer. The trailer opens with the scene of Miles begging the doctors to listen to him. Then it cuts to the new shot. Miles looks at the camera and speaks directly to the audience. "Listen to me," he says. "Please listen! If you don't, if you won't, if you fail to understand, then the same incredible terror that's menacing me will strike at you!"

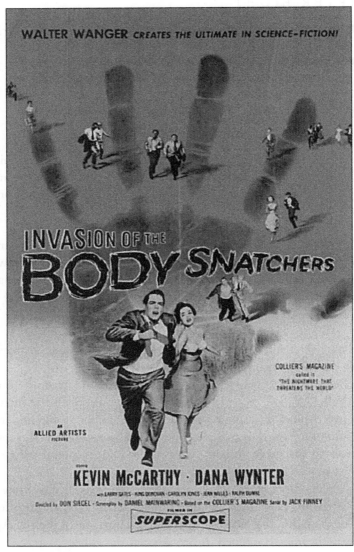

One Sheet Poster.

It was not a novel idea. James Stewart engaged the audience at the opening to the trailer for Alfred Hitchcock's *The Man Who Knew Too Much* that same year. It was a practice that dated all the way back to the 1930s. Actor William Powell stepped off the pages of Dashiell Hammett's novel to introduce *The Thin Man* (1934). Cary Grant, Loretta Young, and David Niven are the trailer for *The Bishop's Wife* (1947). They talk about

This artwork was used on the Style-A Half Sheet Poster and the 24 Sheet Poster.

the movie without showing the audience a single frame from it. *Psycho* (1960) is the ultimate example of this kind of tease. In the trailer, Alfred Hitchcock parades around the sets of his picture, making vague, provocative remarks without revealing any details. It's better than Orson Welles' trailer for *Citizen Kane* (1941).

Deleted scenes and alternate takes were often used in trailers and *The Body Snatchers* contains both. There is the exchange between Miles and Jack about the body on the pool table mentioned in Chapter Six that was deleted from the movie. In the movie, the camera is on Miles and Becky when Danny Kaufman tells them they "have no choice." In the trailer the camera is on Danny. And, of course, there are those scenes of the people running through the streets of Sierra Madre that were filmed exclusively for the trailer.

It's a very good trailer. All of the selling points — Collier's magazine, Dana Wynter, "the sensational star discovery of the *View from Pompey's Head*" and the giant Superscope screen — are highlighted during a collection of scenes that capture the urgency and tension of the movie without revealing too much about it. The trailer department at Allied Artists was

Style A (top) and Style B (bottom) Half Sheet Posters. Style B is the one collectors want the most.

second only to the one at Warner Brothers. I say this as someone who used to collect trailers. Ironically, I never did get my hands on *The Body Snatchers*. I saw it for the first time when Criterion released a laser disc of the movie that included the theatrical trailer. I still haven't seen a television spot. I have to assume it was similar to the other television spots at the time. It probably used some of the same scenes that were in the theatrical trailer, it probably had no music, little, if any, dialogue, with an announcer telling us what we need to know. And there was the usual ten seconds of silent footage at the end to give the local announcer a chance to tell the audience where the picture was playing.

Posters play an important part in selling a picture. Most theatres display posters well in advance of the play date to tickle interest. It's a practice that continues to this day. *The Body Snatchers* posters came in the standard sizes. The 14x22 inch window cards were not used by the exhibitors, but rather were displayed in the windows of the local merchants. The name of the theater was printed on the blank space at the top of these cards. Curiously, the window card is the only poster with the giant alien hands from the newspaper advertisement.

This distorted image of Kevin McCarthy and Dana Wynter was used on the insert poster.

The 11x14 inch lobby cards came in sets of eight and were printed on card stock. Each card featured a hand colored 8x10 inch still with a reproduction of the poster on the left side of the card with the film's title at the bottom. Some studios had what they called a title card which didn't have a still. It was a just the poster. This is the card that is most sought after by collectors. Allied Artists didn't do title cards.

The 40x60 inch posters had a limited run. They were printed on heavy card stock and more often than not were used in public displays, subways being just one example.

The 14x36 inch inserts were also printed on card stock as were the 22x28 half sheets. Often half sheets came in two different styles. The style-A half sheet for the film was a variation of the image that appeared on most of the posters: a large hand print against a red, orange, and yellow background with photograph cut-outs of people running. On each of these posters Kevin McCarthy and Dana Wynter were prominently featured. Style-B was unique. Unlike any of the other posters the background was black. The running figures were captured in spotlights from outer space. This is the poster most sought after by collectors.

This is a publicity still from *Target Earth!* (1954). That's Richard Denning in the background. The woman is Kathleen Crowley with Carolyn Jones' face, an image used for the Style-B Half Sheet.

The rest of the posters — the 41x81 inch three-sheet posters, the 81x81 six sheets posters, the 108x246 inch 24-sheets posters and the 27x41 inch one-sheet posters — were all printed on thin paper stock. The size most often used by theaters around the country was the one-sheet poster. Since it was the most popular size it had the largest print run and is therefore the size most available to collectors. The larger posters were often cut up and used for smaller displays. The 24-sheet posters were for the billboards that lined the public highways.

The art department had to create layouts and finished art that could be used for all of the posters regardless of its size. This wasn't something that was done in-house. The studios made artists compete against each other for the assignment. It was a way getting the best work for the lowest price. Artists were paid as little as $300 for their work, less than they got for magazine illustrations. Images and art were often cut and pasted to fit.

As important as the artwork was, it took a back seat to the concept and the copy. Or so I've been told. For me it was the other way around.

Why the window card for *The Body Snatchers*, with those monster hands, isn't the most sought after by collectors is a mystery to me. That was the art that appeared in most of the newspaper ads and it was also the image on the television slide. "Horror hands," the Exploitation Department called them. Theater owners who wanted to decorate their lobbies with these hands could order them in 27x41 inch sheets in either light green, dark green or magenta at a cost of eighteen cents a sheet. It was just one of the many attention-grabbing suggestions in the press book.

A press book is sort of a do-it-yourself exploitation kit. In addition to showing the exhibitor all of the newspaper ads and posters that were available, it was loaded with promotion gimmicks. Here are a few examples:

SKY-WRITER STUNT

"Invasion of the Body Snatchers" etched into the skies by a sky-writer is a sure-fire and sensational method of attracting attention to this science-fiction thriller. The stunt also suggests the idea of outer-space "invasion." The officials at your nearest airport or landing field will steer you to the right contacts.

LOBBY OR WINDOW STUNT

Place a dummy in a sleeping position on a table, and cover it with a white sheet up to the neckline, with one of the hands suspended over the side so it can be seen by viewers. A dab of red paint (water color), on the palm of the hand will add to the eeriness of the display.

In front of the table spot a good-sized sign bearing the following copy:

FROM THE DOCTOR'S REPORT ON THE "THING" FOUND IN THE BASEMENT. The body on the table was too perfect! IT HAD NEVER BEEN USED! It was never born...never died! Yet it was a man like myself! And if what I was thinking were true ...then the world was faced with a nightmare! SEE 'INVASION OF THE BODY SNATCHERS," STARRING KEVIN MCCARTHY AND DANA WYNTER.

GO AFTER "HORROR" FANS

In many situations, action and horror attractions get the biggest box office returns. "Invasion of the Body Snatchers" contains some very strong moments of fright and suspense, more than enough to satisfy the most avid followers of scary pictures. Here are a few tried and proven angles:

MIDNIGHT SCREENING: Offer a cash award to any women in your town who will accept a challenge to sit all alone through a screening at midnight. Have newspaper follow through with interview, or have radio recording taped to be used on the night before opening.

DARKEN HOUSE: There are many scary moments in the picture which can be made even more eerie by putting your theatre in complete darkness when they are on your screen. When screening your advance NSS [National Screen Service] trailer a dark house will also be very effective.

SPECIAL WARNING POSTER: Have your artist make up a special "horror" 40 x 60 with copy similar to this: WARNING! If you have a weak heart "INVASION OF THE BODY SNATCHERS" is not for you! But if you insist on seeing it, please bring along a bottle of smelling salts…you'll need it! "INVASION OF THE BODY SNATCHERS" is guaranteed to make your blood run cold!

Walter Wanger suggested that Allied Artists give out buttons that said things like: "I don't want to be a pod," "I'm not a pod!" and "Are you a pod?" His idea was as good as any but, like so many of his suggestions, it was ignored.

CHAPTER NINE

THE CRITICS CORNER

Is it necessary for me to say that none of the "respectable" movie critics reviewed *Invasion of the Body Snatchers*? It was predictable. The film had everything going against it. It was a science fiction movie at a time when science fiction movies had about as much prestige as Francis the talking mule. It was also a B-movie which is not to suggest that all B-movies were ignored by the major film critics. But it didn't help. Moreover, there was that title that everyone hated so much. It was an exploitation title, and it was promoted like an exploitation picture. I may be wrong but I believe anyone from *Time* or *Newsweek* or *The New York Times* would have been predisposed to hating the movie just as the trade magazines were to liking it.

Well aware of the stigma attached to his film, Walter Wanger sent a letter to his friend Bosley Crowther, the premier film critic for *The New York Times*, hoping to persuade Crowther to see his picture. I guess he assumed that a favorable review would follow. He suggested that Crowther have Allied Artists send him a copy of the film which was, he said, a plea against conformity. He lamented that the exhibitors didn't think it was right to have an idea in a picture of this sort and hadn't promoted it properly. In spite of this ill treatment, he was happy to report that when some friends of his friends went to see it they couldn't get in because the line was so long. According to *Variety*, it was number nine on their list of top money-makers.

Crowther may have seen the picture but he never reviewed it, which is just as well. His review the following year of *The Incredible Shrinking Man*, one of the best and most exciting sci-fi pictures of the period, was patronizing and derisive. It's doubtful that *The Body Snatchers* would have fared any better. Nevertheless, if you're interested to see what some other people had to say about the film, here are some excerpts of the reviews.

Film Daily, February 28, 1956

Walter Wanger's latest for Allied, a super-duper, science fiction thriller, is exploitable enough to do well in almost any situation. While seemingly tailored for the horror and science fiction markets, "Invasion of the Body Snatchers" bears the mark of careful preparation and expert production values, things which should land it some good play dates. Daniel Mainwaring's careful adaptation of Jack Finney's Collier's serial is suspenseful to the very end, while director Siegel keeps the pace throughout.

Variety, February 16, 1956

...characterizations and situations are sharp as audience interest is enlisted from opening scene. Don Siegel's taut direction is fast-paced generally, although in his efforts to spark the climax he permits his leading character, Kevin McCarthy, to overact in several sequences. Film would have benefitted through more explanatory matter to fully illuminate the scientific premise, but all in all, the topic has been developed along lines to hold the spectator.

Note: When asked to comment on his own performance, Kevin McCarthy admitted that less is more wasn't his strong suit in those days.

The Hollywood Reporter, February 16, 1956, Jack Moffitt

While the mechanics of the plot gimmick are rather sketchily handled in the movie, the actual telling of the story by virtue of Don Siegel's direction, contains a great deal of solid emotion and suspense. The horror is intensified by being played against scenes that are seemingly matter of fact and commonplace.

The suspense holds right up to the final frame and the outcome is more chilling because it is unresolved.

McCarthy has brought his screen style of acting to a high degree of competence in his role of the young doctor. This one is distinctly offbeat.

Note: The three reviews you have just read are all trade publication reviews. Trade magazines exist to support the motion picture industry and as such bend over backwards to find something good to say about every film they review. While their enthusiasm may have been genuine, it is certainly suspect.

Mirror-News, March 1, 1956, Fred W. Fox
It is real escapist entertainment, with the two stars doing most of the escaping. Walter Wanger, a shrewd old-time producer, made the picture for Allied Artists in Superscope. It may have been designed to scare the daylights out of moviegoers, but most of the customers I saw leaving after the show had wide grins. If you like wearies, this one is about as fantastic as you'll find. Daniel Mainwaring did an able job on the screenplay and the action keeps buzzing along.

Los Angeles Examiner, March 1, 1956, Sara Hamilton
...lurking close to the story surface is the suggestion that maybe, in these hectic times, we have subconsciously been hoping for some way out. Some escape from worry and fear. And the unspoken but united mass thought has produced the answer. A VEGETABLE! Scary, isn't it?
Based on a slightly familiar theme (remember *The Thing?*), that of man becoming a plant monster, the tale has been wisely placed by Walter Wanger in a normal, everyday sort of town with normal every day citizens as victims.
The climax is horrific, and if I don't stop looking over my shoulder right now I'll never get through this.
Dan Mainwaring wrote the screenplay and Don Siegel directed. Both lads did an outstanding job.

Note: Sara Hamilton was a former school teacher from Virginia who was once part of Louella Parsons' inner circle, along with Neil Rau. Her glib writing style seems to suggest that Rau had an influence on her. Frankly, I don't think she saw the picture.

Los Angeles Times, March 2, 1956, D.A.
For about two-thirds of length, "Invasion of the Body Snatchers" is a better-than average science-fiction thriller. It has pace, wit, suspense and some sharp acting by its star, Kevin McCarthy.
But just about the time things start getting exciting in this Walter Wanger Pictures, Inc. production, it degenerates into a rather trite, hectic chase with a thoroughly unresolved ending.

Up to this point, Daniel Mainwaring's screenplay, based on a serial by Jack Finney, flashes along with some breezy dialogue and nice pacing. After the plot is uncovered, the dialogue gets windy and the pace too fast for the audience's blood, which is pretty well chilled by this time.

Motion Picture Daily, March 20, 1956

Science fiction emerges as a fine attraction in this Allied Artists melodrama that bears the stamp of originality of producer Walter Wanger. Both he and director Don Siegel make much of mystery, suspense, and superb timing to keep audience interest on a high level from its beginning to its exciting conclusion. Through technical innovations they have removed the film from the basic fantastic fiction class into one that most theatre patrons will brand as "believable."

Daily Film Reviewer, August 23, 1956, F.J.

Brilliant and unusual science shocker for the countless thousands who enjoy being chilled to the marrow. In Superscope.

The horrors and build-up of tension are extraordinarily well done in this film. But what gives it an added value is its explicit warning of the ever-present danger of losing our humanity and turning into a passionless automaton with the mere outward semblance of a human being. "Humanity is never more precious than when you are in danger of losing it" is the moral of the story — and a very worthwhile one too.

Kevin McCarthy is excellent in the main role. The others have less to do, but Dana Wynter is decorative and the supporting cast convincing.

An outstanding product of its kind.

London trade magazine, undated, M.M.W.

Plot is thoroughly extravagant but holds together firmly and maintains a super-high level of tension, aided by very perceptive direction and excellent photography and lighting. Incident is ingeniously contrived and the performance of stars and supports accord exactly with the story's nightmare mood. Contrasting this mood effective are the very humdrum small-town settings. As entertainment, this is just about as offbeat as you can get, but the film ranks with the few best science-fiction subjects.

This Walter Wanger production, under Don Siegel's direction, never puts a foot wrong. The build-up is carefully timed, with a strong element of mystery as well as mounting tension and the tragic love interest is developed with restraint. The ultimate horror of the story becomes almost unbearable and then, like all nightmares, it ends abruptly.

The British poster was similar to the American newspaper advertisements.

Monthly Film Bulletin, October 1956

An expert and off-beat science-fiction thriller…The main fault lies in the weakly drawn characterization of hero and heroine; there are signs of an attempt to give them a fuller background — they are lifelong friends and each has had a previous unhappy marriage — but these aspects remain on the level of statements and, in particular, the colourless playing of Dana Wynter constitutes a drawback. Also, the reasons and ambitions of the "Things" are only perfunctorily explained and the rhythm of the chase through the tunnel is curiously muffled. But, in the main, this is a persuasive thriller, with excellent atmospheric lighting in the night scenes and a commendably concession less ending.

As you can see, the reviews at the time were mostly favorable.

When the smoke cleared (according to *Variety*) the film grossed $1,200,000 domestically, which was pretty tidy profit for Allied Artists. It was released in West Germany and Sweden in May of the following year. It wasn't seen in Turkey until 1958. On November 8, 1967 it finally found its way to France where it was re-released in 2009.

In 1962 a distribution company called National Telefilm Associates (NTA) acquired the rights to *The Body Snatchers*. They were the ones who released it to television. Later, after buying the name and trademarks of the old Republic Pictures studio, NTA changed its name to Republic Pictures Corporation in 1986. They were purchased by Spelling Entertainment in 1994. The video rights to their library were leased to Artisan Entertainment. Viacom bought the portion of Republic that Spelling didn't own and now Republic is a division of Paramount. Artisan was sold to Lions Gate Home Entertainment. Does that mean Lions Gate owns the picture or only part of it?

NTA held the last copyright. So where does this leave *The Body Snatchers*? In a paraphrase of Danny Kaufman's line from the film, "Whose film was it and where is it now?"

A few years ago historian Bill Warren, author of the wonderful *Keep Watching the Skies*, was involved in a new DVD release of the movie. Kevin McCarthy and Dana Wynter did a commentary track for it. It included a documentary with McCarthy visiting some of the locations. So what happened to it? Five will get you ten nobody knows who owns what anymore. My advice to all of you fans is to hold onto those old Republic DVDs.

CHAPTER TEN

THE REMAKES

BY GARY A. SMITH

By 1978, the major studios were well aware of the box office potential of horror, fantasy, and science fiction. No longer relegated to "B" movie status, sci-fi movies were given bigger budgets and wider distribution, and were made by people who grew up loving the old B sci-fi movies. *Jaws* (1975), *Star Wars* (1977), and *Close Encounters of the Third Kind* (1977) made unprecedented millions. The studios began searching for other fantastic subject matter to bring to the motion picture screen.

Producer Robert H. Solo, a former talent agent and the producer of *Scrooge* (1970) and *The Devils* (1971), had long been a fan of *Invasion of the Body Snatchers*, although he was unaware that it had ever been a novel at the time. Shortly before the mid-seventies big budget sci-fi/horror boom, he paid $10,000 of his own money to option the rights to the novel and the original film. His plan was, more or less, to do a straightforward remake in color. He didn't care for the ending of the original picture. He thought it was a cop out and a joke, as if the FBI could save the world. He finally read the novel and thought he might do something similar to what Finney had in mind.

W.D. Richter, the writer of *Slither* (1973), *Peeper* (1975) and *Nickelodeon* (1976) was hired to script the project and Philip Kaufman, the director of *Goldstein* (1964), *Fearless Frank* (1967), *The Great Northfield Minnesota Raid* (1972) and *The White Dawn* (1974) were brought into the project. Richter's first draft was set in a small town on the outskirts of San Francisco. Two months into preproduction, the producer, the director and the writer were in a meeting. Solo stepped out of the room to go to the bathroom and by the time he got back, Kaufman and Richter decided the film would be more interesting if it took place in San Francisco. Although Kaufman loved the original film, he wanted his version to be more contemporary. He also wanted to make it clear to the audience from the beginning, unlike the original, that it was a science fiction picture. This decision to shift the story from a small town to the big city so late in the game made it necessary for Richter to rewrite it as it was being made. The film became a re-imagining of the Walter Wanger version rather than a remake.

Solo took his project to Warner Bros. but they passed on it. He ended up making a deal with United Artists. Of course, with the typical hubris of anyone who undertakes the remaking of a classic film, Solo announced at the time that the premise of *The Body Snatchers* had taken on ramifications more pertinent and chilling than those of twenty years ago. His version would not be a sequel, but use the earlier version as "a point of departure for a fascinating and frightening new film."

Well, sort of.

During the opening credits, life forms floating from a distant dying planet fall in a rainstorm onto San Francisco. These gossamer shapes quickly develop into blossoming flowers which proliferate throughout the city's vegetation and San Francisco, a city known for nonconformity, becomes the center of an invasion based on conformity of the worst kind.

The lead character suffers a downgrade in stature in this new version. While Miles Bennell was a medical doctor in the original film, his counterpart, Matthew Bennell, is an inspector for the Department of Public Health who spends his time looking for rat turds in the kitchens of fancy restaurants. His co-worker, Elizabeth Driscoll, suspects that her boyfriend, Geoffrey, isn't really Geoffrey anymore.

Given the film's larger budget, the special effects are more extravagant and yucky but they are never quite as creepy as those in the original version. This is particularly true of the unformed Jack Belicec double, herein found in a sauna mud bath rather than on a pool table. The most memorable special effect in the film occurs when Matthew and Elizabeth are confronted with a pod's botched attempt to duplicate a street singer and his dog, the result being a hideous man-headed canine.

The major set pieces of the first movie are retained with the most effective aspects of the 1978 version being the sequences which are closest to the source. But this film sorely lacks the fast pacing of the original. One detail, which was not in the original version, is the high-pitched howl that the pod people emit whenever they are "outing" a real human. Although this was obviously meant to be frightening, it ends up being as annoying as the Daleks' voices in *Doctor Who*.

The acting ranges from quite good (Brooke Adams) to downright awful (Jeff Goldblum), with Donald Sutherland somewhere in between, offering a bland performance in the lead.

In knowing nods to the original, Kevin McCarthy and Don Siegel appear in cameo roles. Siegel is a sinister cab driver and McCarthy is again running through the streets shouting "They're here! They're here!"

Brooke Adams and Donald Sutherland in a scene from Philip Kaufman's remake of *Invasion of the Body Snatchers.*

as if he never stopped running from the previous picture. A homeless man, who'd been watching the action from the curb, called to McCarthy when he was finished with the scene. "Wasn't you in the first one?" he asked McCarthy. The actor told him that he was. "That one was better," the man told him. McCarthy fell down laughing.

Jack Finney was invited to appear in the film in a scene with Leonard Nimoy, but the author declined. He was angry that he hadn't been paid for the use of his story but the fact of the matter was he'd sold the rights to Allied Artists back in 1955.

Robert Duvall, who had previously been in director Philip Kaufman's *The Great Northfield Minnesota Raid,* appears here in a brief scene as a priest on a swing.

The film was extremely popular with audiences and critics alike. Many people like it as well or better than the original. It did manage to retrieve the kind of shock ending that Siegel had originally wanted. With a budget of about three and a half million dollars it grossed over eight times its cost in the United States alone. Its success helped pave the way for other big budget "B' movie remakes such as *The Thing* (1982) and *The Fly* (1986). Unfortunately the film doesn't hold up particularly well. The "new age" atmosphere has caused it to date far more than the original version.

Body Snatchers (1994), is the least remembered version of the three, but has the distinction of taking the premise of the book in an interesting new direction. Originally conceived as a sequel to Solo's previous film. This time Warner Brothers wanted in on the action. What the studio and the producer hoped to do was create a Body Snatchers franchise. Instead it turned into a nightmare, especially for Solo who left the film business afterwards.

Steve Malone is a scientist who works for the Environmental Protection Agency. He is sent to a remote Army base in Alabama to check out levels of toxic waste. His teenage daughter Marti resents the move. She is uncomfortable around her stepmother, Carol, and isn't particularly fond of her young half-brother, Andy. On their way to the base, the family stops at a gas station where Marti is accosted in the rest room by a soldier who tells her "They get you while you sleep." It won't take viewers long to realize that those pesky pods are at it again.

The plot is largely original although some of the elements from both previous versions are preserved ("Don't show any emotion. They can be fooled.") Unfortunately, that annoying alien howl from the second film is back again. The scope of the invasion has once again been narrowed, confined to an Army base. In earlier drafts of the script the intention was for the military to move the invasion on to Washington D.C.

Larry Cohen was hired to write the screenplay for this youth-oriented take on Finney's story. He was quite familiar with science fiction, having developed *The Invaders* television series back in 1967. For the big screen he wrote *It's Alive* (1974) and the sequel *It Lives Again* (1978). He both wrote and directed *Q* (1982) and *The Stuff* (1985). Solo thought Cohen's script was pretty good, but there was a regime change at Warner Brothers and the new executive assigned to the picture didn't like it. He hired Stuart Gordon, who'd directed a series of low budget horror films for Charles Band, among them the widely popular *Re-Animator* (1985), *From Beyond* (1986), *Dolls* (1987), *The Pit and the Pendulum* (1991) and the futuristic sci-fi film *Robot Jox* (1990). Gordon brought in his buddy,

Dennis Paoli, to help him. Gordon soon found himself in "development hell." According to Solo the script went through five writers and twenty-five drafts. Gordon jumped ship when he was offered another project and was replaced by Abel Ferrara, fresh from his critically lauded movie *The Bad Lieutenant* (1992). Solo thought that Ferrara was a poor choice and the two were continually at odds during the shooting.

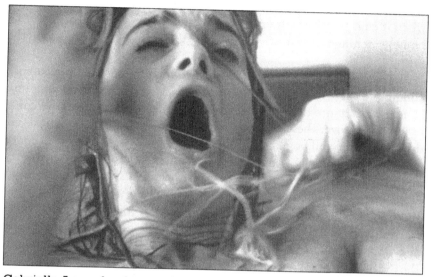

Gabrielle Anwar has issues with the pods in this scene from *Body Snatchers*, a completely new take on Jack Finney's story.

Thomas Burman, who had done the effects for the previous remake, had less to do this time around. Ferrara's idea was to keep the sci-fi elements to a minimum. The main sequence involving the pods occurs while Marti is soaking in a hot bath. She falls asleep and a pod, placed in the ceiling over the bathtub by army personnel, sends forth tentacles which begin to cover her body and enter into her nostrils and mouth. Fortunately she wakes in the nick of time, only to have the partially formed duplicate fall on her when the ceiling collapses.

Other memorable sequences include soldiers harvesting pods from the swamps at night and an infirmary where sleeping patients lie in one bed as their duplicates takes form in the bed beside them.

In spite of the fact that Ferrara managed to make a pretty scary film, Warner executives weren't happy with it. It didn't test well, so they were going to send it straight to video. On his own, Ferrara entered it in the Cannes Film Festival where it got good reviews, which led to a theatrical release in France. The studio was shamed into giving it a theatrical release in the U.S., but they never really got behind it. With a budget of $13 million, the movie grossed a meager $428,868 domestically and put an end to any thoughts about a franchise.

Last but certainly not least, we come to the next (and so far final) version of Finney's story, simply titled *The Invasion*. Apparently not having learned its lesson, Warner Bros. had this project in the works back in 2004 when it engaged David Kajganich to write the screenplay. This time the body-snatching aliens finally made it to Washington D.C. but not in the form of pods.

A space shuttle crashes on Earth with a membranous alien substance clinging to the wreckage. This substance transforms anyone coming into contact with it into the emotionless, mindless "pod people" we have come to know and love. These infected humans spread the contagious virus via drinking water and bogus flu inoculations.

When psychiatrist Carol Bennell's patients claim their loved ones aren't really their loved ones anymore (a suspicion she's harbored about her own ex-husband), she he wonders if maybe she's been right all along. The trouble is that he has their young son Oliver for the weekend.

In this version, the alien infiltration is successfully squelched by producing a vaccine gleaned from people who had scarlet fever as children. The movie also exploits the current obsession with protecting "the children" from any disaster, major or minor, real or imaged. The thought seems to be that if a situation is scary, add a child in peril and it will be even scarier (think Steven Spielberg's *War of the Worlds*). This attitude differs significantly from the Ferrara version where a "pod child" is thrown screaming from a helicopter in flight.

Director Oliver Hirschiegel was given a 45-day shooting schedule. Like Don Siegel, he decided to eschew elaborate visual effects and concentrate on the suspenseful aspects of the story. Warner executives were not pleased. They hired Laurence and Andrew Wachowski (creators of *The Matrix* films) to re-write the script and shoot additional footage. The film languished for over a year before director Jim McTeigue was hired to do 17 more days of re-shoots. The film was released to audience and critical indifference. The $65 million-dollar film grossed a bit over $40 million.

Despite their inflated budgets and technological advances, not *one* of the subsequent versions of *The Body Snatchers* comes close to being as good as the original. And the moral of this story is: If it ain't broke, don't fix it. Or remake it.

Invasion of the Body Snatchers
December 1978

PRODUCER: Robert H. Solo DIRECTOR: Philip Kaufman SCREEN-PLAY: W.D. Richter MUSIC: Denny Zeitlin PHOTOGRAPHER: Michael Chapman EDITOR: Douglas Stewart PRODUCTION DESIGNER: Charles Rosen MAKEUP: Thomas R. Burman SPECIAL EFFECTS: Russ Hesey and Dell Rheaume.

CAST: Donald Sutherland *(Matthew Bennell)*, Brooke Adams *(Elizabeth Driscoll)*, Leonard Nimoy *(Dr. David Kibner)*, Veronica Cartwright *(Nancy Belicec)*, Jeff Goldblum *(Jack Belicec)*, Art Hindle *(Geoffrey)*, Lelia Goldoni *(Katherine)*, Tom Luddy *(Ted Hendley)*, Stan Ritchie *(Stan)*, David Fisher *(Mr. Gianni)*, Tom Dahlgren *(Detective)*.

RUNNING TIME 115 minutes. RELEASED BY United Artists.

Body Snatchers
January 1994

PRODUCER: Robert H. Solo DIRECTOR: Abel Ferrara SCREEN-PLAY: Stuart Gordon, Dennis Paoli, Nicholas St. John, STORY: Raymond Cistheri, Larry Cohen MUSIC: Joe Delia PHOTOGRAPHER: Bojan Bazelli EDITOR: Anthony Redman PRODUCTION DESIGNER: Peter Jamison.

CAST: Gabrielle Anwar *(Marti Malone)*, Terry Kinney *(Steve Malone)*, Meg Tilly *(Carol Malone)*, Reilly Murphy *(Andy Malone)*, Bill Wirth *(Tim Young)*, Christine Elise *(Jenn Platt)*, R. Lee Ermey *(Gen. Platt)*, Kathleen Doyle *(Mrs. Platt)*, Forest Whitaker *(Maj. Collins)*.

RUNNING TIME 87 minutes. RELEASED BY Warner Bros.

The Invasion
August 2007

PRODUCER: Joel Silver DIRECTOR: Oliver Hirschiegel SCREEN-PLAY: David Jajganich MUSIC: John Ottman PHOTOGRAPHER: Rainer Klausmann EDITOR: Joel Negron, Hans Funck PRODUCTION DESIGNER: Jack Fisk.

CAST: Nicole Kidman *(Carol Bennell)*, , Daniel Craig *(Ben Driscoll)*, Jeremy Northam *(Tucker Kaufman)*, Jeffrey Wright *(Dr. Stephen Galeano)*, Veronica Cartwright *(Wendy Lenk)*, Jackson Bond *(Oliver)*, Josef Sommer *(Dr. Henryk Belicec)*, Celia Watson *(Ludmilla Belicec)*.

RUNNING TIME 99 minutes. RELEASED BY Warner Bros.

Kevin McCarthy.

BIOGRAPHIES

KEVIN McCARTHY
(FEBRUARY 15, 1914-SEPTEMBER 11, 2010)

Won acclaim in the 1949 London stage production of Arthur Miller's *Death of a Salesman*. He played the role of the disenchanted son, Biff Loman, which he later he reprised in Stanley Kramer's 1951 film version. He got an Oscar nomination for that film. He was hailed as the Golden Globe "New Star of the Year." During a career that spanned half a century, he appeared in dozens of feature films, over 160 television shows and 30 made-for-TV movies. For years he toured with the successful one-man stage show, *Give 'Em Hell, Harry!* Yet, much to his surprise, it was *The Body Snatchers* for which he was best remembered. In the late 1970s, during a question and answer session following a screening of the film at the Leo S. Bing Theatre, director Don Siegel told the audience that the film owed a great deal of its impact to McCarthy's performance. McCarthy, sitting in a chair next to him, dryly remarked: "If that's the case why didn't you ever use me again?"

Born in Seattle, Washington, McCarthy was orphaned at the age of four when his parents, Martha Therese Preston and Roy Winfield McCarthy, died in the 1918 flu epidemic. The four McCarthy children were taken in by relatives of their grandmother and after five years of what Kevin's sister, Mary, described as near-Dickensian mistreatment, Mary went to live with their grandparents and the boys were placed in a Catholic boarding school.

A self-described ne'er-do-well with low self-esteem, McCarthy found himself living on five-cent White Tower hamburgers and five-cent O'Henry bars after his uncle, fed up with the young man's sloth, gave him the shoe. McCarthy enrolled in a couple of correspondence courses at the University of Minnesota and was surprised when he passed. He became a full-time student and made the Dean's List. It was Larry Gates, the actor who played Danny Kaufman in *The Body Snatchers*, who persuaded McCarthy to try out for the school production of *Henry IV*. That was when McCarthy discovered that he enjoyed acting. He moved to New York and made his Broadway debut in Robert E. Sherwood's' Pulitzer Prize-winning drama, *Abe Lincoln in Illinois*. In 1947, together with Lewis and Cheryl Crawford, Elia Kazan and Karl Malden, McCarthy founded the famous Actor's Studio.

McCarthy loved acting and he loved to work. When he wasn't on stage he was on screen, in movies and television, a larger than life actor often playing larger than life roles. In the early 60s he did commercials for Ipana toothpaste and twenty years later he was the spokesman for Firestone Tires. There were life-sized cut-outs of him in every showroom.

I finally got to chat with Kevin McCarthy at some length on the set of *Ghoulies Go to College* (1990). Like so many film fans who have an affair with this movie or that, I wanted impress on him just how much *The Body Snatchers*, and his performance in it, meant to me, as if it could or should have made a lick of difference to him. He thanked me but I could tell that he was simply being polite, that I hadn't gotten through to him. We talked about the picture and some of the other movies that I'd seen him in. I knew he was friends with Montgomery Clift so we talked about Clift for a while. Then my friend Bob Villard took a picture of us together and McCarthy went back to work. Bob and I hung around for about an hour or so and were on our way out when McCarthy called to me from across the stage. "Hey! Mark!" he yelled. "Thanks. Thanks for what you said." I was higher than a kite.

He was married twice, first to actress Augusta Dabney in 1941 (for twenty years) and later to lawyer Kate Crane. He had five children, three by his first wife, two by his second.

In the 1990s, when he learned that fans were paying as much as $25 a pop for autographs at movie poster shows, McCarthy phoned Dana Wynter in Ireland to tell her about it. He left the following message on her answer machine: "Becky, it's Miles. Wake up!"

McCarthy died at Cape Cod Hospital in Hyannis, Mass.

Movies include: *Drive a Crooked Road, The Gambler from Natchez* (1954); *Stranger on Horseback, An Annapolis Story* (1955); *Nightmare* (1956); *Diamond Safari* (1958); *The Misfits* (1961); *40 Pounds of Trouble* (1962); *A Gathering of Eagles, An Affair of the Skin, The Prize* (1963); *The Best Man* (1964); *Mirage* (1965); *A Big Hand for the Little Lady* (1966); *Hotel* (1967); *The Hell with Heroes* (1968); *If He Hollers, Let Him Go!, Ace High* (1968); *Kansas City Bomber* (1972); *Buffalo Bill and the Indians*

(1976); *Piranha* (1978); *Hero at Large* (1980); *The Howling* (1981); *Inner Space* (1987); *Fast Food, UHF* (1989); *Love or Money, The Sleeping Car* (1990); *Final Approach* (1991); *The Distinguished Gentleman* (1992); *Matinee* (1993); *Greedy* (1994); *Just Cause* (1995); *Looney Tunes: Back in Action* (2003); *Loving Annabelle, Fallen Angels* (2006); *Slipstream* (2007); *Her Morbid Desires* (2008); *Wesley* (2009)

TV Shows include: *The Ford Theatre Hour, Actor's Studio* (1949); *Studio One in Hollywood, Pulitzer Prize Playhouse, The Prudential Family Playhouse* (1950); *The Ford Television Theatre, Lights Out* (1952); *Danger* (1953); *Ponds Theater, Inner Sanctum, Goodyear Playhouse, Omnibus* (1954); *The United States Steel Hour, Star Tonight, Matinee Theatre, Schlitz Playhouse* (1955); *Star Stage, Front Row Center, Telephone Time* (1956); *The 20th-Century Fox Hour, Crossroads, Cavalcade of America, Kraft Theatre, Climax,* (1957); *The DuPont Show with June Allison* (1959); *Twilight Zone* (1960); *Armstrong Circle Theatre, Way Out, Great Ghost Tales, Ben Casey* (1961); *Target: The Corrupters, Going My Way, The Rifleman* (1962); *The Defenders, Breaking Point, Dr. Kildare* (1963); *Mr. Novak, The Alfred Hitchcock Show, Burke's Law* (1964); *Honey West* (1965); *The Fugitive, The Man from U.N.C.L.E, 12 O'Clock High, Bob Hope Presents the Chrysler Theatre, Felony Squad, The F.B.I.* (1966); *The Road West, The Invaders, Garrison's Gorillas, Judd for the Defense* (1967); *Hawaii Five-O, The Wild, Wild West, The Name of the Game, The High Chaparral, The Guns of Will Sonnett* (1968); *The Survivors* (1969); *Julia* (1970); *Mission: Impossible* (1971); *Between Time and Timbuktu, A Great American Tragedy, Banacek* (1972); *Columbo* (1973); *Great Performances, Cannon* (1974); *The Seagull, Order to Assassinate* (1975); *Eco-Man, Mary Jane Harper Cried Last Night* (1977); *Portrait of an Escort, Flamingo Road* (1980); *Rosie, The Rosemary Clooney Story* (1982); *Amanda's, Making of a Male Model, The Love Boat, Bay City Blues* (1983); *Fantasy Island, Invitation to Hell, Dynasty* (1984); *Deadly Intentions, Scarecrow and Mrs. King, Hotel, Murder She Wrote, The Midnight Hours* (1985); *A Masterpiece of Murder, The Colby's, The A-Team, The Golden Girls, Fame* (1986); *Home, LBJ: The Early Years, Square One, Poor Little Rich Girl: The Barbara Hutton Story, The Long Journey Home, Head of the Class* (1987); *In the Heat of the Night, Simon & Simon* (1988); *Passion and Paradise, China Beach, Matlock* (1989); *The Rose and the Jackal* (1990); *Father Dowling Mysteries, Dead on the Money, Charlie Hoover* (1991); *Duplicates, Human Target, Batman, Tales from the Crypt* (1992); *Rebel Highway, Roadracers, Dream On* (1994); *Liz: The Elizabeth Taylor Story, The Sister-in-Law* (1995); *Boston Common* (1996); *Early Edition, Elvis Meets Nixon, The Weird Al Show* (1997); *The District* (2000)

Dana Wynter.

DANA WYNTER
(JUNE 8, 1931-MAY 5, 2011)

Born Dagmar Wynter in Berlin. She lived in England until her surgeon father moved the family to Southern Rhodesia when she was 16. She was the only female student at Rhodes University where she studied medicine and dabbled in theatrics. By the time she returned to England acting had trumped doctoring. She got a few bit parts in a handful of British films but it was her stage work that caught the attention of an agent. He brought her to New York in 1953. She changed her name to Dana (pronounced "Donna"). After living on doughnuts for several months she got a break when Eva Gabor dropped out of the lead role in an episode of the *Robert Montgomery Presents* television series. Her work in live television (which she preferred to movies) led to a seven year contract with 20th Century Fox. The starting date of that contract was postponed so that she could appear in *The Body Snatchers*.

On her way to work on *The Body Snatchers* one morning, Wynter found a pod on her doorstep, left there by the film's director, Don Siegel, who was courting the woman who lived next door. It had the effect that Siegel had hoped it would.

Miss Wynter hasn't seen *The Body Snatchers* since she made it and she'd just as soon not think about it. Although she was happy to have been a part of it, it isn't something that she's proud of because she thought she was boring in it. Because of her lack of experience, she didn't think her performance had the edge it needed.

Her first Fox film was *The View from Pompey's Head* (1956). Of her films, the one she liked best was the wartime romance *D-Day, the Sixth of June* (1956).

Miss Wynter died from congestive heart failure in Ojai, California. She was buried in Ireland where she built a home after making the movie *Shake Hands with the Devil* (1959).

Movies include: *Night Without Stars, White Corridors, Lady Godiva Rides* (1951); *Something Money Can't Buy, The Woman's Angle, It Started in Paradise, The Crimson Pirate* (1952); *Colonel March Investigates, Knights of the Round Table* (1953); *Something of Value* (1957); *In Love and War, Fraulein* (1958); *Sink the Bismarck!* (1960); *On the Double* (1961); *The List of Adrian Messenger* (1963); *If He Hollers, Let Him Go!* (1968); *Airport* (1970); *Santee* (1973).

TV Shows include: *Suspense, The United States Steel Hour* (1954); *Studio One, The 20th Century Fox Hour* (1955); *Colonel March of Scotland Yard* (1956); *Playhouse 90* (1957-59); *Wagon Train* (1961-64); *The Dick*

Powell Theatre , Whatever You Do, Don't Panic — unsold pilot (1962); *The Virginian, Burke's Law* (1963); *12 O' Clock High* (1964-66); *Kraft Suspense Theatre, The Alfred Hitchcock Hour, The Rogues, Convoy, Run for Your Life* (1965); *The F.B.I.* (1966), *Gunsmoke* (1967); *The Name of the Game* (1968); *It Takes a Thief, Get Smart, Love American Style, Ironsides* (1969), *Marcus Welby, M.D.* (1971); *Hawaii Five-O* (1972), *Cannon* (1973), *McMillan and Wife* (1974), *Ellery Queen* (1976), *Backstairs at the White House, The Rockford Files* (1979), *Hart to Hart* (1981), *Magnum P.I.* (1982).

LARRY GATES
(1915-1996)

Won an Emmy Award for playing H.B. Lewis on the daytime soap, *Guiding Light*, from 1983 to 1995. Throughout his career he often played lawyers and judges. But he was happiest playing comedy on stage. In 1963 he was nominated for a Tony Award for his role in the courtroom drama *A Case of Libel*.

Gates was studying chemical engineering at the University of Minnesota when he started acting in student productions. In 1938, he moved to New York to be an actor. During an audition for the Barter Theater he tripped and fell flat on his face. He got back on his feet and continued his performance without missing a beat. Laurette Taylor, considered by many to have been one of the most influential stage actresses, was watching. She told him that he was stark raving mad but an actor if she ever saw one. He made his debut one year later in *Speak of the Devil*.

Gates appeared in the Broadway productions of *Cat on a Hot Tin Roof*, *The Teahouse of the August Moon*, and *Bell, Book and Candle*.

In the 1950s, he and his wife Judy made the little town of Cornwall, Connecticut their home. Gates died from leukemia in 1996 and thirteen years later, a few months after his wife's death, the town learned that the couple had left them a $200,000 donation.

Movies include: *Glory Alley* (1952); *Francis Covers the Big Town* (1953); *The Girl Rush* (1956); *The Strange One, Jeanne Eagles, The Brothers Rico* (1957); *Cat on a Hot Tin Roof, Some Came Running* (1958); *The Great Imposter, Hoodlum Priest, The Young Savages, Ada* (1961); *Toys in the Attic* (1963); *The Sand Pebbles* (1966); *In the Heat of the Night, Hour of the Gun* (1968); *Airport* (1970); *Funny Lady* (1975).

TV Shows include: *Goodyear Playhouse* (1953); *Kraft Theatre* (1955); *The Alcoa Hour, Studio One, Hallmark Hall of Fame* (1957); *Armstrong Circle*

Theatre, The Untouchables (1960); *Alfred Hitchcock Presents, One Step Beyond, Twilight Zone* (1961); *Kraft Mystery Theatre, Saints and Sinners* (1962); *The Defenders* (1963); *Slattery's People, 12 O'Clock High* (1965); *The Invaders, Judd for the Defense* (1968); *Banyon* (1972); *The F.B.I.* (1973); *Mannix, The Missiles of October* (1974); *Lou Grant* (1978); *Backstairs at the White House* (1979); *F.D.R.: The Last Year* (1980).

Kevin McCarthy, Larry Gates, and King Donovan.

KING DONOVAN
(JANUARY 25, 1918-JUNE 30, 1987)

Was often cast in comedic roles. I remember watching him on *The Bob Cummings Show* where he played the hen-pecked Harvey Helm in 17 episodes. He was very funny. He was also a regular on *The Burns and Allen Show* and played Herb Thorton, the next-door neighbor on *Please Don't Eat the Daisies*. But Donovan was a capable dramatic actor as well.

His career began at The Butler Davenport Theater on 63rd Street in New York City. He was a teenager then. During the 1940s he toured with the Jitney Players and finally, in 1948, he landed a part in a Broadway show, *The Vigil*. That same year he was cast as a bigoted gang member in the low budget film, *Open Secret*. Two of his biggest roles were in science fiction pictures — *The Magnetic Monster* (1953) and *The Body Snatchers*.

Donovan enjoyed a modest career in features and television shows, always returning to the theater between assignments. He met his wife-to-be, Imogene Coca, when they appeared together in the 1958 Broadway production of *The Girls* in 509. Like Donovan, she was the offspring of vaudevillian parents. The couple appeared in more than 30 shows together.

In 1963 actor-turned-producer Tommy Noonan hired Donovan to direct his low-budget, black and white nitwit comedy *Promises! Promises!* The film's sole raison d'être was the "promise" of seeing actress Jayne Mansfield in the altogether. The film was promoted in the pages of *Playboy* magazine and made some money, but it did nothing for Donovan's directing career. He helmed four episodes of his wife's short-lived TV show, *Grindl*, and one episode of *That Girl*. After completing a nine-month tour with the show *On the Twentieth Century*, he was taken by cancer.

Movies include: *Open Secret, Man from Texas* (1948); *Alias Nick Beal, All the King's Men* (1949); *A Lady Without Passport* (1950); *The Enforcer, Little Big Horn, Angels in the Outfield, His Kind of Woman* (1951); *Sally and Saint Anne, The Merry Widow* (1952); *The Beast from 20,000 Fathoms, Forever Female, Half a Hero, Easy to Love, Tumbleweed* (1953); *Riders to the Stars* (1954); *The Seven Little Foys* (1955); *The Birds and the Bees* (1956); *The Iron Sheriff* (1957); *Cowboy, The Defiant Ones, I Want to Live!* (1958); *The Perfect Furlough, The Hanging Tree* (1959); *Nothing Lasts Forever* (1984).

TV Shows include: *The Life of Riley, Private Secretary* (1953); *Four Star Playhouse* (1954); *Schlitz Playhouse of Stars, Medic, Cavalcade of America, Lux Video Theatre* (1955); *It's a Great Life, December Bride, Adventures of Wild Bill Hickok* (1956); *The Adventures of Jim Bowie, Playhouse 90, Navy Log, Tales of Wells Fargo, The Gale Storm Show* (1957); *Bat Masterson, Wagon Train, Alcoa Theatre, Trackdown* (1958); *77 Sunset Strip, Wanted: Dead or Alive, Richard Diamond, Private Detective, Mr. Lucky, Riverboat, Maverick* (1959); *Bonanza, Shotgun Slade* (1960); *Rawhide, Arrest and Trial* (1963); *The Defenders* (1965); *The Big Valley, The Smothers Brothers Show, Daktari* (1966); *The Beverly Hillbillies* (1967).

CAROLYN JONES
(APRIL 28, 1930-AUGUST 3, 1983)

Won the Golden Globe Award in 1958 for being one of the three most promising newcomers after appearing in dozens of TV shows and films. Just the year before, she'd been nominated for an Academy Award for her role as the sad and lonely floozy in Paddy Chayefsky's *The Bachelor Party*. (The Academy has a history of giving awards to women who play floozies and whores.) So she was anything but a newcomer.

Jones was very good in that role, but she was even better as Shirley Drake, the once-hopeful -actress-turned theatrical agent in the 1959 film *Career*. She was good in almost everything she did.

Growing up in Amarillo, Texas, she dreamed of coming to California to enroll in the Pasadena Playhouse. Her grandparents gave her the money to do it. After graduating from the Playhouse, Jones went through a complete surgical make-over. It worked. She caught the eye of a talent scout from Paramount while she was performing at the Players Ring. She was signed to a six-month contract. Her first screen appearance was in the studio's crime-fighting drama, *The Turning Point* in 1952. When her contract expired, she went to work in television. Pneumonia forced her to turn down the role in *From Here to Eternity* that Donna Reed earned an Academy Award for. That same year she appeared in Warner Bros. 3-D scare film, *House of Wax*, and married Aaron Spelling, who at that time was a struggling actor. He eventually became a successful producer and Carolyn appeared in an episode of his popular *Fantasy Island* TV show in 1977, eleven years after the couple had divorced.

It was in television where Miss Jones finally came into her own, playing Morticia Addams on the popular network series, *The Addams Family* (1964-1966), for which she received a Golden Globe nomination.

In 1971 she wrote *Twice Upon a Time*, a novel about an actress from Texas. She was diagnosed with colon cancer shortly after she went to work on a daytime CBS soap opera, *Capitol* (1981). As the cancer spread she was forced to play her part in a wheelchair. She died in her West Hollywood home at the age of 53.

Movies include: *Road to Bali* (1952); *Off Limits, The Big Heat* (1953); *Make Haste to Live, The Saracen Blade, Shield for Murder, Three Hours to Kill, Desiree* (1954); *The Seven Year Itch, The Tender Trap* (1955); *The Man Who Knew Too Much, The Opposite Sex* (1956); *Baby Face Nelson* (1957); *Marjorie Morningstar, King Creole* (1958); *The Man in the Net, A Hole in the Head, Career, Last Train from Gun Hill* (1959); *Ice Palace* (1960); *Sail a Crooked Ship* (1961); *How the West Was Won* (1962); *A Ticklish Affair* (1963); *Heaven with a Gun, Color Me Dead* (1969); *Eaten Alive* (1977).

TV Shows include: *The Pepsi-Cola Playhouse, Four Star Playhouse* (1954); *Meet Mr. McNulty; Treasury Men in Action, Dragnet, Alfred Hitchcock Presents, Studio 57* (1955); *The 20th Century-Fox Hour, State Trooper,* (1956); *Panic!, G.E. Theatre, Climax!, The Millionaire, Schlitz Playhouse* (1957); *Playhouse 90* (1958); *The David Niven Show* (1959); *The DuPont Show* (1960); *Zane Grey Theatre* (1961); *Dr. Kildare, The Dick Powell Theatre* (1962); *Wagon Train, Burke's Law, The DuPont Show of the*

Week (1964); *Batman* (1966), *The Danny Thomas Hour* (1967); *Brackens World*, *The Mod Squad* (1969); *The Name of the Game* (1970); *Dan August* (1971); *Circle of Fear* (1972); *The New Perry Mason* (1973); *Ironside* (1974); *Kolchak: The Night Stalker* (1975); *Ellery Queen* (1976); *Roots*, *The New Adventures of Wonder Woman*, *Halloween with the New Addams Family* (1977); *The Love Boat* (1979); *The Dream Merchants* (1980); *Quincy M.E.*, *Midnight Lace*.

JEAN WILLES
(APRIL 15, 1923-JANUARY 3, 1989)

Was born Jean Donahue in Los Angeles but grew up in Salt Lake City, Utah. She made her feature debut in the 1942 Paramount film *So Proudly We Hail* and found steady work in a series of Columbia shorts with comedians such as Harry Langdon, Andy Clyde, and The Three Stooges, often working without screen credit. She changed her name in 1947.

Possibly because she exuded sexuality, she was often typecast as hard-boiled floozies and appeared mostly in television and B-movies. When she was able to land a role in an A-movie it was usually in a small part. She married NFL football player Gerald Cowhig in 1951 and the two remained married until her death from liver cancer in her Van Nuys home in 1989.

Movies include: *Here Come the Waves* (1944); *Salty O-Rourke*, *Incendiary Blonde* (1945); *Blondie Knows Best* (1946); *Blondie in the Dough* (1947); *A Woman of Distinction*, *Kill the Umpire*, *David Harding*, *Counterspy*, *The Petty Girl*, *The Fuller Brush Girl*, *Revenue Agent* (1950); *Jungle Jim in the Forbidden Land* (1952); *The Sniper*, *Son of Paleface*, *Torpedo Alley* (1952); *Abbott and Costello Go to Mars*, *Run for the Hills*, *From Here to Eternity*, *The Glass Web* (1953); *Masterson of Kansas* (1954); *Bowery to Bagdad*, *5 Against the House*, *Count Three and Pray* (1955); *The Lieutenant Wore Skirts*, *The Revolt of Mamie Stover*, *Toward the Unknown*, *The King and Four Queens* (1956); *The Man Who Turned to Stone*, *The Tijuana Story*, *Hell on Devil's Island* (1957); *Desire Under the Elms*, *These Thousand Hills* (1958); *Elmer Gantry*, *Ocean's Eleven*, *The Crowded Sky* (1960); *By Love Possessed* (1961); *The Cheyenne Social Club* (1970); *Bite the Bullet* (1975).

TV Shows include: *Boston Blackie* (1951); *The Range Rider*, *Four Star Playhouse*, *I'm the Law*, *The Ford Television Theatre*, *Adventures of Superman* (1953); *Mr. & Mrs. North*, *The Adventures of the Falcon*, *The Mickey Rooney Show*, *The Pepsi-Cola Playhouse*, *G.E. Theatre*, *The Jack Benny Program* (1954); *The Lone Wolf*, *The Lineup*, *Medic*, *Stories of the Century*, *Four Star Playhouse*, *The Man Behind the Badge*, *The George Burns and Gracie Allen*

Show, Science Fiction Theatre, Tales of the Texas Rangers (1955), *It's a Great Life, Crossroads, Wyatt Earp, Screen Directors Playhouse, The Adventures of Dr. Fu Manchu, Zane Grey Theater, Studio 57* (1956); *The New Adventures of Charlie Chan, The Gray Ghost, The Adventures of McGraw, State Trooper, Perry Mason, Man Without a Gun, Tales of Wells Fargo, Goodyear Theatre* (1957) *Whirlybirds, M Squad, Maverick, Richard Diamond, Colt .45, Tombstone Territory, Mike Hammer, Frontier Doctor, Bat Masterson, The Millionaire, Lawman, Wanted: Dead or Alive* (1958); *The Rough Riders, The Texan, Zorro, Bronco, The Man from Blackhawk, Bonanza* (1959); *Wagon Train, Hawaiian Eye, Surfside 6* (1960); *Peter Gunn, Twilight Zone* (1961); *Cheyenne* (1962); *McHale's Navy, Empire, The Alfred Hitchcock Hour, Temple Houston, 77 Sunset Strip* (1963); *Death Valley Days, The Beverly Hillbillies* (1965); *The Virginian, T.H.E. Cat* (1966); *The Guns of Will Sonnett* (1967); *Here's Lucy* (1970); *Kojak* (1975); *The Blue Knight* (1976).

RALPH DUMKE
(JULY 25, 1899 — JANUARY 4, 1964)

Was born in South Bend, Indiana and studied law at Notre Dame where he met another wanna-be actor, Charles Butterworth. The two became fast friends and were responsible for a number of campus shows.

Dumke was in Vaudeville and radio before breaking into the movies in 1942. He was Captain Andy in the 1946 Broadway revival of the musical *Showboat*, a role he reprised in the early television series Captain Billy's *Mississippi Music Hall* (1947).

He died of a heart attack at the age of 64 in Sherman Oaks, California.

Movies include: *Lucky Jordan* (1942); *All the King's Men* (1949); *Where Danger Lives, Mystery Street, The Breaking Point, The Fireball* (1950); *When I Grow Up, The Law and the Lady, The Mob* (1951); *Boots Malone, Carbine Williams, The San Francisco Story, We're Not Married, Hurricane Smith* (1952); *The Mississippi Gambler, Lili, Count the Hours, The President's Lady, The War of the Worlds* (1953); *It Should Happen to You, Alaska Seas, She Couldn't Say No, They Rode West, Rails to Laramie, Massacre Canyon* (1954); *Violent Saturday, Daddy Long Legs, Hell's Island, The Desperate Hours, Artists and Models* (1955); *Forever Darling, Francis in the Haunted House, The Solid Gold Cadillac* (1956); *Loving You, The Buster Keaton Story* (1957); *Wake Me When It's Over, Elmer Gantry* (1960); *All in a Night's Work* (1961).

TV Shows include: *China Smith* (1952); *Racket Squad, My Little Margie* (1953); *Waterfront* (1954); *TV Reader's Digest, Fireside Theatre, Father Knows Best, The Ford Television Theatre* (1955); *Studio 57, Climax!,*

Producer's Showcase (1956); *I Love Lucy, The George Burns and Gracie Allen Show* (1957); *Walt Disney Presents: Annette, The Gale Storm Show, Shirley Temple Theatre, The Real McCoys* (1958); *Lassie, The Texan, Bachelor Father, Perry Mason, Dennis the Menace* (1959); *Rawhide, The Andy Griffith Show* (1961).

VIRGINIA CHRISTINE
(MARCH 5, 1920–JULY 24, 1996)

I was at a screening of *The Body Snatchers* once when the audience burst into laughter at the first close-up of Virginia Christine. They weren't ready to accept her as Wilma Lentz. For 21 years, beginning in 1965, she'd been Mrs. Olsen, the friendly, coffee-peddling neighbor on the Folgers' TV commercials. She had, at that point, *become* Mrs. Olsen, so much so that in 1971 the folks in Stanton (her hometown) made the city's water tower look like a giant coffeepot. But horror fans remember her best as Princess Anaka in Universal's *The Mummy's Curse* (1944), rising out of a Florida swamp, twitching and jerking, covered with gook and old age makeup. The actress told movie historian Greg Mank that they saved that shot for the last day of shooting "so in case they killed me off, everything would be in the can!" The blond actress donned a black wig for the role. "I thought I was smashing!"

Born in Iowa, her real name was Virginia Kraft. In high school she won a National Forensic League award which led to a gig on a Chicago radio station. When the family moved to Los Angeles, she continued to work in radio while attending the University of California. She studied dancing with Maria Bekefri, was a trained lyric soprano, a concert pianist, and spoke French, Swedish, and German.

She was signed to a two-year contract with Warner Brothers after a talent scout saw her in a play at the Hollywood Playhouse. The Playhouse was a showcase for young hopefuls, owned and operated by German actors Joseph Schildkraut and Fritz Feld. (She married Feld in 1940.) But Warners didn't seem to know what to do with her. She fared better at Universal with a meaty part in *The Killers* (1946).

She was a regular on TV's *Tales of Wells Fargo* (1961–1962) as Ovie Swenson and though she worked steadily she never had the career that she deserved. Mrs. Olson was more or less a consolation prize.

She died from heart disease at the age of 76.

Movies include: *Edge of Darkness, Mission to Moscow, Action in the North Atlantic* (1943); *Phantom of the Plains, Girls of the Big House, Counter-Attack* (1945); *The Scarlet Horseman, Murder is My Business, House of Horrors, The*

Wife of Monte Cristo (1946); *The Invisible Wall, The Gangster* (1947); *Cover Up* (1949); *The Men, Cyrano de Bergerac* (1950); *High Noon* (1952); *Never Wave at a WAC, Woman They Almost Lynched* (1953); *The Cobweb, Not as a Stranger, Good Morning, Miss Dove* (1955); *The Killer is Loose, Nightmare, Three Brave Men* (1956); *The Spirit of St. Louis, Johnny Tremain, The Careless Years*, (1957); *Flaming Star* (1960); *Judgment at Nuremberg* (1961); *The Prize, 4 for Texas* (1963); *A Rage to Live* (1965); *Billy the Kid vs. Dracula* (1966); *Guess Who's Coming to Dinner* (1967); *In Enemy Country* (1968).

TV Shows include: *Front Page Detective* (1951); *Dragnet* (1952); *I'm the Law, Four Star Playhouse* (1953); *Adventures of Superman, The Ford Television Theatre, The Whistler* (1954); *Studio 57, Alfred Hitchcock Presents* (1955); *Father Knows Best, Front Row Center, Private Secretary, Science Fiction Theatre, G.E. Theatre; The Adventures of Jim Bowie* (1956); *State Trooper, Hey, Jeannie, The Lone Ranger, Matinee Theatre, Gunsmoke* (1957); *Whirlybirds, Mike Hammer, The Restless Gun, The Millionaire, The Thin Man, Peter Gunn, Zane Grey Theatre* (1958); *Wanted: Dead or Alive, The Loretta Young Show, Rescue 8, Steve Canyon, The Lawless Years, Frontier Doctor, How to Marry a Millionaire, The DuPont Show with June Allison, Twilight Zone, The Rifleman* (1959); *M Squad, Riverboat, 77 Sunset Strip, The Untouchables, Rawhide, Thriller* (1960); *Perry Mason, Wagon Train, Shirley Temple Theatre, Maverick, The Deputy, Mister Ed* (1961); *The New Breed, Target: The Corrupters, Stoney Burke* (1962); *The Eleventh Hour* (1963); *The Fugitive, Ben Casey, The Killers, Hazel* (1964); *The Virginian, Bonanza, Wagon Train, The Big Valley* (1965); *The F.B.I.* (1966); *The Invaders* (1967); *Daniel Boone* (1968); *Lancer, Daughter of the Mind* (1969); *Nanny and the Professor, The Old Man Who Cried Wolf* (1970); *Ironside* (1976); *Kojak* (1978); *Scooby-Doo and Scrappy-Doo* (1979).

WHIT BISSELL
(OCTOBER 25, 1909-MARCH 6, 1996)

When I was a kid I went to the movies almost every week and watched way too much TV for my own good, and it seemed like I saw Whit Bissell at least once, sometimes two or three times a week. This may be an exaggeration but not much of one. Forget all of the movies he was in. If you just watched television you couldn't miss him. He was in three episodes of *Science Fiction Theatre* (1955-56). He was a regular on *Bachelor Father* (1958-60). And it seemed like he got at least one shot on every Western series (and in the 1950s, Westerns were about all that was on TV; he was on *The Rifleman* four times!). In the 1960s he was a regular on *Peyton Place* (1965) and *The Time Tunnel* (1966-67). By the time I met him at his home in the summer of 1982, he'd been married three times and had two daughters. I interviewed a lot of people and I don't think anyone made me feel more at home than Whit Bissell. I kept calling him Mr. Bissell until put his hand on my shoulder and said, "The name is Whit." He couldn't remember all of the films I wanted to talk about. He was in so many and may have only worked a day or two on some of them. (It's like asking a plumber about a house he worked on 30 years ago.) He was a little embarrassed when I mentioned *Teenage Frankenstein* (1957). With a shrug of his shoulders he said, "You've done it and you can't very well say you didn't do it. You're caught with your pants down, so to speak." But when I brought up *The Body Snatchers* he smiled. "Now I thought that was a pretty good picture, didn't you?"

His real name was Whitner Nutting Bissell, the second of five children, born in New York City. His parents, James and Helen Bissell, sent him to private schools. He majored in English and Drama at the University of North Carolina where he trained with the Carolina Playmakers. He later joined the Civic Repertoire Company in New York and The National Theatre Company after that. He had appeared in a number of Broadway shows by the time he entered the movies in 1943. I saw one of his last stage appearances, a production of *12 Angry Men* at the Henry Fonda Theatre in Hollywood.

Parkinson's disease took his life in 1994. He was buried in the Westwood Village Memorial Park Cemetery in Los Angeles.

Movies include: *Holy Matrimony, Destination Tokyo* (1943); *Winged Victory* (1944); *Cluny Brown, Brute Force, A Double Life* (1947); *Raw Deal, He Walked by Night* (1948); *Anna Lucasta, Tokyo Joe* (1949); *Side Street, Wyoming Mail, The Killer That Stalked New York* (1950); *The Red Badge of Courage, Sealed Cargo, Lost Continent* (1951); *Boots Malone, Skirts Ahoy!, The Sellout* (1952); *Devil's Canyon, It Should Happen to You, Riot in Cell Block 11* (1953); *Creature from the Black Lagoon, The Caine Mutiny, Target Earth* (1954); *The Big Combo, Not as a Stranger, The Desperate Hours* (1955); *The Proud Ones, Man from Del Rio* (1956); *The Young Stranger, Gunfight at the O.K. Corral, I Was a Teenage Werewolf, Johnny Tremain* (1957); *The Defiant Ones, Monster on the Campus, The Black Orchid* (1958); *Warlock, No Name on the Bullet, Never So Few* (1959); *The Magnificent Seven, The Time Machine* (1960); *Birdman of Alcatraz, Hemingway's Adventures of a Young Man, The Manchurian Candidate* (1962); *Spencer's Mountain, Hud* (1963); *Seven Days in May, Advance to the Rear, Where Love Has Gone* (1964); *Fluffy, The Hallelujah Trail* (1965); *Airport* (1970); *Pete 'n' Tilly* (1972); *Soylent Green* (1973); *Casey's Shadow* (1978).

TV shows include: *The Web, Studio One* (1952); *The Pepsi-Cola Playhouse, G.E. Theatre* (1954); *The Halls of Ivy, Climax! You Are There, Cavalcade of America, Studio 57, The 20 Century-Fox Hour* (1955); *Zane Grey Theatre, Schlitz Playhouse, The Ford Television Theatre, Father Knows Best* (1956); *Playhouse 90, The Gale Storm Show, Panic! Cheyenne, Alcoa Theatre, The Restless Gun, Tales of Wells Fargo, M Squad* (1957); *Sea Hunt, The Thin Man, Have Gun Will Travel, State Trooper, The Real McCoys, Peter Gunn, Lawman, Wagon Train* (1958); *The Texan, Rawhide, The Millionaire, The Lineup, The Untouchables, Men Into Space* (1959); *Hawaiian Eye, Bourbon Street Beat, Route 66, Perry Mason, The Roaring 20s, Maverick, Surfside 6* (1960); *The Tom Ewell Show, The Law and Mr. Jones, The Bob Cummings Show, The Detectives* (1961); *Alfred Hitchcock Presents, Bonanza* (1962); *The Virginian, The Dakotas, The Donna Reed Show, The Outer Limits* (1963); *Kraft Suspense Theatre, Ben Casey, Profiles in Courage* (1964); *Dr. Kildare, Daniel Boone, Mr. Novak, Voyage to the Bottom of the Sea* (1965); *The F.B.I., Laredo, The Man from U.N.C.L.E., Hogan's Heroes, I Dream of Jeannie* (1966); *Gomer Pyle, U.S.M.C., The Iron Horse, Star Trek* (1967); *Judd for the Defense, The Name of the Game* (1968); *Here's Lucy, The Mod Squad, Mannix, Julia* (1969); *Land of the Giants, It Takes a Thief, The Andersonville Trial, The Young Lawyers* (1970); *City Beneath the Sea, Cannon, In Broad Daylight, O'Hara, U.S. Treasury* (1971); *The Bold Ones, Ironside, Barnaby Jones, Cannon, Cry Rape* (1973) *The F.B.I. Story, Lincoln Crossing Fox River* (1974); *Harry O, Matt Helm, Psychic Killer* (1975); *Flood!, Kojak* (1976); *The Tony Randall Show, Last of the Mohicans, The Bionic Woman* (1977); *Donner Pass, Quincy M.E., Project U.F.O.* (1978); *The Incredible Hulk, Ike, The War Years* (1979); *The Dukes of Hazzard* (1980); *Walking Tall* (1981); *Hart to Hart* (1982); *Emerald Point N.A.S.* (1983); *Falcon Crest* (1984).

CARMEN DRAGON
(JULY 28, 1914-MARCH 28, 1984)

Was born and raised in Antioch, California to a musical family. He graduated from San Jose College with an MA degree and began his musical career with Meredith Willson's orchestra as an arranger. He was the conductor of the Hollywood Bowl Orchestra for ten years and the Glendale Symphony for 20 years. In 1945, he won an Oscar (with Morris Stoloff) for his score of *Cover Girl* and began writing music for radio and television.

In my fifth grade class, during music appreciation, we listened to some classical music radio program. When the announcer said the orchestra was conducted by Carmen Dragon I was delighted. Suddenly, the music had special meaning to me. He recorded at least 70 albums for Capital Records. In 2004, The Antioch Unified School District named one of its new elementary schools in his honor. He died of cancer in St. John's Hospital in California.

Don Siegel didn't care for Carmen Dragon's score for *The Body Snatchers*. He said it was too much. Maybe it was but I like it. I can't imagine the film without it.

Film credits include: *Mr. Winkle Goes to War* (1944); *Young Widow, The Strange Woman* (1946); *Dishonored Lady, Out of the Blue* (1947); *Kiss Tomorrow Goodbye* (1950); *Night into Morning, The Law and the Lady, The People Against O'Hara* (1951); *When in Rome* (1952); *At Gunpoint* (1955).

TV credits include: *Dr. Kildare* (1961).

DANIEL MAINWARING
(FEBRUARY 27, 1902 — JANUARY 31, 1977)

Began his writing career at the San Francisco Chronicle, first as a copy boy and later a journalist. He was working as a crime reporter at the Los Angeles Examiner when he published his first novel in 1932, *One Against the Earth*. As Geoffrey Holmes (his two middle names) he wrote a series of detective novels. While he was working as a publicist at Warner Bros, he wrote six pictures in one year for producer Bill Thomas (of Pine-Thomas) at Paramount. In 1947, he wrote the screenplay for RKO's now classic *Out of the Past* (1947) based his novel *Build My Gallows High*. He didn't get credit for the screenplay he wrote for *The Hitch-Hiker* (1953) nor did get all of the money that he was promised. Ida Lupino, the film's director, kept half of his money and took the credit herself. She told him there was nothing he could do about it. Dannie and Deborah, Mainwaring's daughters, told this story. Exactly why Miss Lupino thought she could get away with this crummy behavior isn't clear. Perhaps she knew that Mainwaring was fronting for blacklisted writers at the time. Maybe she would have blown the whistle on him if he had raised a stink.

When things started slowing down for him in the 1960s, Mainwaring wrote English language versions of Italian sword and sandal movies. Most of his other work during this period was in television. Director Joseph Losey, who shared Mainwaring's nostalgia for small town life, thought he was an underrated writer and a noble man.

Mainwaring's personal favorites of the films he wrote were *Out of the Past* and *The Lawless* (1950), a film about the mistreatment of migrant fruit pickers in Central Valley. The author grew up in the San Joaquin Valley and had picked fruit as a child. He'd seen the racism and abuse first hand.

Movies include: *Secrets of the Underground* 1942; *Dangerous Passage* (1944); *Tokyo Rose* 1945; *They Made Me a Killer, Hot Cargo, Swamp Fire* (1947); *Roughshod, The Big Steal* (1949); *The Eagle and the Hawk* (1950); *The Tall Target, The Last Outpost, Roadblock* (1951); *Bugles in the Afternoon, This Woman is Dangerous* (1952); *Powder River, Those Redheads from Seattle* (1953); *Alaska Seas, Southwest Passage, The Desperado, Black Horse Canyon* (1954); *Tormenta, A Bullet for Joey, An Annapolis Story* (1955); *Thunderstorm* (1956); *Baby Face Nelson* (1957); *Cole Younger, Gunfighter, The Gun-Runners, Space Master X-7* (1958); *Walk Like a Dragon* (1960); *Atlantis, the Lost Continent* (based on a 1945 play by Gerald Hargreaves), *The George Raft Story* (1961); *Convict Stage, The Woman Who Wouldn't Die* (1965).

Television Shows include: *General Electric Summer Originals* (1956); *The Californians* (1958); *Adventures in Paradise* (1959); *Outlaws* (1960); *Cain's Hundred, Target: The Corrupters* (1962); *A Man Called Shenandoah* (1965); *The Wild, Wild West, Custer* (1967); *Cimarron Strip, Mannix* (1968).

JACK FINNEY
(OCTOBER 2, 1911-NOVEMBER 14, 1995)

Was awarded a Special Prize from *Ellery Queen's Mystery Magazine* for his first published short story, "The Widow's Walk," in spite of the fact that it contained no mystery, no detective, and no crime. He was living in New York at the time, married to Marguerite Guest and working for an advertising agency. He moved to California in the early 1950s and settled in Mill Valley, the setting for *The Body Snatchers*.

Finney wrote both short stories and novels, often with protagonists so bored with their lives that either they turn to crime or retreat into the past through self-hypnosis or some other time travel device. Several of his stories were made into motion pictures and television shows. *Such Interesting Neighbors* was filmed twice, as "Time is Just a Place" on *Science Fiction Theatre* (1955) and again under its original title on *Amazing Stories* (1987). "All of My Clients Are Innocent" (1959) was a 1962 episode of *Alcoa Premier. The Love Letter* (1959) was the basis for a 1987 *Hallmark Hall of Fame* movie. And although I can find no mention of it, sometime in the 50s I remember seeing a half hour TV adaptation of his short story "Of Missing Persons."

In 1987, he was given the World Fantasy Award for Life Achievement at the World Fantasy Convention in Nashville, Tennessee. His last novel was *From Time to Time* (1995), a sequel to his popular *Time and Again* (1970).

The author was amused by the "deep" meaning that Walter Wanger and Don Siegel found in *The Body Snatchers*. The idea that he would write an entire novel just to say that individuality was a good thing was (to use my own expression) prepodsterous.

Jack Finney died of pneumonia and emphysema in Greenbrae, California.

Novels include: *Five Against the House* (1954); *The Body Snatchers* (1955); *The House of Numbers* (1957); *Assault on a Queen* (1959); *Good Neighbor Sam* (1963).

Short Story Collections include: *The Third Level* (1957); *I Love Galesburg in the Springtime* (1963); *Forgotten News: The Crime of the Century and Other Lost Stories* (1983); *About Time* (1986); *Three by Finney* (1987).

Short Stories include: "Cousin Len's Wonderful Adjective Cellar", "Breakfast in Bed" (1948); "Something in the Clouds" (1949); "I'm Scared" (1951); "Second Chance" (1956); "Home Alone" (1961); "Hey, Look at Me!" (1962); "The Woodrow Wilson Dime" (1968).

WALTER WANGER
(JULY 18, 1894–NOVEMBER 17, 1968)

Graduated from Dartmouth College where he was active in the theatre. His management skills caught the attention of English producer who had come to America to create a National Theatre. He hired Wanger to help him run things. It wasn't long before Wanger was producing his own successful stage productions, which ultimately led to his being hired by Paramount executive Jesse Lasky.

For nine years, Wanger served as Paramount's general manager. When Lasky resigned, Wanger was fired and he went to work for Columbia Pictures, Metro-Goldwyn-Mayer, and returned to Paramount as an independent producer. In 1936, he signed a 10-year contract with United Artists and produced a string of hit movies. He was active in the Motion Picture Relief Fund and served as president of The Academy of Motion Picture Arts and Sciences.

Fed up with the way things were run in Hollywood, he joined independent producers Charlie Chaplin, Walt Disney, Samuel Goldwyn, Alexander Korda, Mary Pickford, David Selznick and Orson Welles to form The Society of Independent Motion Picture Producers (SIMPP) whose members believed that the only way creativity could flourish in Hollywood was by eliminating the studio system. These were the only people who supported Wanger when he was arrested for shooting his wife's lover, Jennings Lang.

After his release from prison, the only place he could find work was at Allied Artists. He made two successful low budget features for them and was back in the big leagues with *I Want to Live* (1958), a powerful drama that netted Susan Hayward an Oscar. It is unfortunate that his next project was the ill-fated *Cleopatra* (1963). The trials and tribulations surrounding the production of that film have been well documented. Everything that could have gone wrong did. The $2 million dollar budget swelled to an astronomical $44 million and threatened to throw Fox into bankruptcy. Wanger was fired and never made another picture. He died five years later from a heart attack. Don Siegel called him a "rarity" among producers. He encouraged creativity and wasn't simply interested in protecting himself, which, Siegel said, is what most producers do.

Movies include: *The Lady Lies* (1929); *The Bitter Tea of General Yen, Gabriel Over the White House* (1933); *Queen Christina* (1933); *Shanghai* (1935); *The Trail of the Lonesome Pine, The Case Against Mrs. Ames* (1936); *Algiers, Trade Winds* (1938); *Stagecoach* (1939); *Sundown* (1941); *Arabian Nights* (1942); *Gung Ho!* (1943); *Salome Where She Danced, Scarlet Street* (1945); *Canyon Passage* (1946); *Smash-Up: The Story of a Woman, The Lost Moment* (1947); *Tap Roots, Joan of Arc* (1948); *Tulsa, Reign of Terror, The Reckless Moment* (1949); *Lady in the Iron Mask* (1952); *Kansas Pacific, Fort Vengeance* (1953); *Riot in Cell Block 11, The Adventures of Haji Baba* (1954); *Navy Wife* (1956).

DON SIEGEL
(OCTOBER 26, 1912-APRIL 20, 1991)

Referred to himself as a whore because he took every assignment that came along, which explains why most of his movies aren't about anything. He thought *The Body Snatchers* was his best picture.

Siegel's vaudevillian parents were teaching music when Siegel was born in Chicago. A Cambridge University graduate, he was introduced to producer Hal Wallis by an uncle (Jack Saper) who had been a film editor at Warner Bros. He went to work in the studio's film library, became an assistant editor and finally the head of the montage department. He broke out of the montage prison when he was allowed to direct two short subjects — *Star in the Night* and *Hitler Lives!* — and walked away with two Academy Awards.

Don Siegel quickly earned a reputation for getting the most from the least and became what is known as an action director. He had two rules that he lived by: Start the movie fast and under budget so the front office will leave you alone. And shoot only what you need so they can't screw it up too badly later on.

After a series of tough and gritty crime dramas Siegel's career hit a slump. He turned to television. His first TV movie, *The Killers* (1964), was considered too violent for television. It was released theatrically.

It was his association with Clint Eastwood that propelled Siegel back to the big screen. Eastwood said he learned a lot about directing from Siegel and dedicated *Unforgiven* (1992) to him.

In 1981 Siegel retired, after a horrendous experience with Bette Midler on the movie *Jinxed!* The director said he'd let his wife, children and animals starve before he'd subject himself to something like that again. Ten years later, he died from cancer in Los Angeles. When asked what he thought of Siegel, Kevin McCarthy said he liked the S.O.B. in spite of his sardonic streak. For beneath Siegel's crusty, saturnine exterior, McCarthy saw a heart of gold.

Movies include: *The Verdict* (1946); *Night Unto Night* (1947); *The Big Steal* (1949); *Duel at Silver Creek* (1952); *China Venture* (1953); *Riot in Cell Block 11, Private Hell 36* (1954); *An Annapolis Story* (1955); *Crime in the Streets* (1956); *Baby Face Nelson, Spanish Affair* (1957); *The Gun Runners, The Lineup* (1958); *Hound Dog Man, Edge of Eternity* (1959); *Flaming Star* (1960); *Hell is for Heroes* (1962); *The Killers* (1964); *Coogan's Bluff, Madigan* (1968); *Two Mules for Sister Sara* (1970); *The Beguiled, Dirty Harry* (1971); *Charley Varrick* (1973); *The Black Windmill* (1974); *The Shootist* (1976); *Telefon* (1977); *Escape from Alcatraz* (1979); *Rough Cut* (1980).

TV shows include: *The Lineup* (1954); *Frontier* (1955); *Adventure Showcase* (1959); *Alcoa Theatre* (1960); *Bus Stop* (1961); *The Lloyd Bridges Show, Breaking Point, Twilight Zone* (1963); *Destry, The Hanged Man* (TV movie), *Convoy, The Legend of Jesse James* (1965).

SELECTED BIBLIOGRAPHY

Boddy, William. "Daniel Mainwaring." *Dictionary of Literary Biography*, vol. 44, American Screenwriters, 2nd set, pp. 207-215, Detroit: Gail Research Co., 1986.

Kaminsky, Stuart M. *American Film Genres*. New York: Dell. 1977.

King, Stephen. *Stephen King's Danse Macabre*. New York: Everett House, 1981.

La Valley, Al. *Invasion of the Body Snatchers, Don Siegel Director*. New Jersey: Rutgers University Press, 1989.

Lovell, Alan. *Don Siegel, American Cinema*. London. British Film Institute, 1975.

Gorman, Ed and Kevin McCarthy. *"They're Here..." Invasion of the Body Snatchers. A Tribute*, pp 63-68, 187-273. New York: Berkely Blvd Books, 1991.

Schneider, Jerry L. *Invasion of the Body Snatchers Film Locations: Then & Now*. Corriganville Press, 2009.

Smith, Steven C. *Film Composers Guide*, pp 185. California: Lone Eagle Publishing Co. 1990.

Warren, Bill. *Keep Watching the Skies! The 21st Century Edition*, pp 419-426. McFarland & Co., Inc., 2010.

SELECTED BIBLIOGRAPHY

INDEX

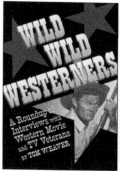

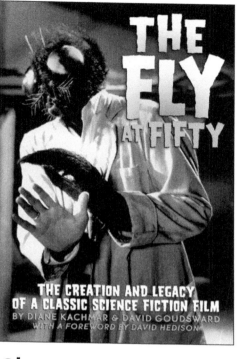

Lightning Source UK Ltd.
Milton Keynes UK
UKOW06f0603300117
293174UK00016B/515/P